MEMOIRS OF A PARTY ANIMAL

ANIMAL

Seven Decades in Animal Welfare

by

ANGELA HUMPHERY

with Liz Hodgkinson

To Wonaid Chris hover liels Perey + Ayek 5·12·14

First Printing: 2014

Cover picture by Mike Lawn

Back cover image by kind Permission of cartoonist Ken Pyne

ISBN 978-1-326-06891-2

Contents

This book is dedicated to...

Percy the 'Galgo' (Spanish Greyhound), Joey the Capuchin Monkey and Oliver the Moon Bear.

These three animals were rescued from a fate worse than death and adopted by me, although only Percy lives with us.

It is also dedicated to the wonderful people I have met and made friends with in animal welfare, who have dedicated their lives to making the world a better place for all creatures great and small.

Virginia McKenna, OBE, founder of Born Free Foundation.

Dr Jill Robinson, MBE, Founder of Animals Asia Foundation.

Alan Knight, OBE, Founder of International Animal Rescue.

Pen Farthing, Founder of Nowzad Dogs.

Gavin and Andrea Boulger, Founders of Wetnose Animal Aid.

Ira Moss, Founder of All Dogs Matter.

Marc Abraham, Founder of Pupaid.

Anne Finch, Founder of Greyhounds in Need.

My husband Martin Humphery, current Chairman of Greyhounds in Need.

Peter Egan, actor and friend of animals.

Joh Rendall, owner of Christian the lion and Trustee of the George Adamson Wildlife Preservation Trust.

The late Kate Hosali, founder of SPANA (Society for the Protection of Animals) and current Chief Executive, Jeremy Hulme.

The late Dorothy Brooke, Founder of The Brooke Hospital.

The late Juanita Carberry, feisty friend, shipmate and champion of animals.

I love parties. I love animals.
But not necessarily in that order. I've been holding parties since the age of ten to raise funds for animals so I suppose I am that mythical beast – a party animal.

FOREWORD

Mahatma Gandhi once said, 'The morality of a country is judged by the way it treats its animals.' Animal welfare or, you could say, animal cruelty, is a can of worms. Worldwide, animals are exploited daily – hunted, shot, trapped, snared, skinned alive or caged in zoos and circuses, incarcerated in laboratories and factory farms while the long-haul transport and ritual slaughter of food animals accounts for the suffering of millions more.

The dog, said to be 'man's best friend', fares no better. Puppy farming – intensive breeding of puppies for profit - is rife in the UK while strays around the world are being shot or poisoned. In the Mediterranean this is done at the end of the summer when the tourists have gone home and there is nobody left to feed the dogs.

The problem of strays is particularly acute in Romania. I have seen pictures online of a shelter there, with wheelbarrows piled high with dead dogs. Dogs they had just killed, euthanased, put down, gone long walkies or whatever you like to call it. There is a bounty for the tail of a dead dog, so great is the problem, and dogs are brutally killed in the streets by anyone out to make a fast buck. This wholesale massacre is a national disgrace.

The credit crunch and recession has had a devastating effect on animal shelters in the UK as well, with twice the number of animals coming in but only half the money. Many unwanted family pets are given the kiss of death with a lethal jab, their owners unable to afford their upkeep. Horses, too, are dumped in the countryside because of the high cost of fodder and veterinary fees and needless to say, these large animals are twice as hard to rehome as a cat or a dog. With so many unwanted horses, is it any wonder they are all too likely to end up in the food chain?

Wildlife the world over is currently in crisis too; at tipping point we might say. The poaching of rhino and elephant in Africa to satisfy the insatiable demand for horn and ivory in South East Asia is now bringing these two great species to the brink of extinction. So dire is the situation that Tanzania's Tourism Minister has demanded an official shoot-to-kill policy in their national parks against elephant poachers, estimating that between 30 and 70 adult elephants are being killed every day for their tusks, while across Africa some 25,000 wild elephants are being killed every year.

At this current scale of slaughter the African elephant could die out in the wild within 50 years.

Although this shoot-to-kill policy has elicited protests from Human Rights groups, the UK-based charity, Care for the Wild International, says, 'the stakes are so high now, and the potential profits so great, that unless the poachers know the risks that are involved, they are not going to stop.' In 2013, a Vietnamese man was arrested at Nairobi airport with 20k of rhino horn, which fetches up to twice its weight in gold. Rhino horn is widely touted as a cure for impotence, which of course it is not. Horn is made up of keratin as are our nails. If only men would bite their nails or stick to Viagra perhaps we could save the rhino.

Reports in The Daily Mail and Sunday Telegraph in October 2013 revealed that poachers in Zimbabwe have killed more than 300 elephants and countless other safari animals by cyanide poisoning, planting buckets of water laced with the poison in sand at waterholes in the 5,660-square mile Hwange National Park. Carnivores such as lions and hyenas feeding on the carcasses died too. Allegedly villagers sell elephant tusks for £300 each to cross border traders who then resell them in South Africa for £10,000 a pair. The Born Free

Foundation has sent out an urgent appeal, 'ELEPHANT EMERGENCY – ONE KILLED EVERY 15 MINUTES.' I never thought to see that in my lifetime.

How wonderful then that Prince William, Duke of Cambridge, highlighted the plight of these two great giants at the Tusk Conservation Awards held in London on 12 September 2013 at The Royal Society and has pledged himself to wipe out ivory hunting, even going so far as to say he would like to destroy all the ivory carvings in Buckingham Palace.

An added bonus for Tusk Trust, which I support, and of which Prince William is patron, is that it was the first time Kate and Wills had been seen out in public since the birth of their son, Prince George. Kate looked so stunning in her sequined gown that it wasn't too surprising that the event was given worldwide coverage. William's involvement has brought this ghastly trade into mainstream news media everywhere.

How ironic is it then that while the number of rhino, elephant and even lion, is shrinking by the minute there are far too many dogs and certainly far too many humans. That thought was expressed long ago by D.H. Lawrence in his 1920s poem, Mountain Lion, where two Mexicans have killed a mountain lion just for the hell of it:

And I think in the world beyond, how easily we might spare a million or two humans and never miss them. Yet what a gap in the world, the missing white frost-face of that slim yellow mountain lion!

Sir David Attenborough has recently made this point: 'There is no environmental problem facing our planet that would not be easier to solve if there were fewer people, and no problem that does not become harder – and ultimately impossible to solve – with ever more.' He was vilified for saying as much about the human population's continuing explosion while a friend of mine jokingly remarked, 'perhaps we need a human cull. What about people burgers?'

Being so passionate about the animal world but not being a vet and therefore unable to work in this field, the only avenue open to me for helping was to become a supporter of animal welfare charities, not only raising funds but raising awareness and spreading the word with all the means at my disposal.

Since becoming a PDSA Busy Bee as a child, my family (as I like to think of them) has grown enormously, encompassing almost every species. I now support about 50 animal charities including big well known ones such as the PDSA, RSPCA, RSPB, WSPA, WWF-UK, Battersea Cats' and Dogs' Home, Blue Cross, World Horse Welfare, Horse Trust and Dogs Trust, Wood Green, Compassion in World Farming and People for the Ethical Treatment of Animals (PETA.)

I also help some of the smaller ones such as The Monkey Sanctuary, Greek Animal Welfare Fund, Redwings Horse Sanctuary, Bransby Horses and the Environmental Investigation Agency as well as the Gorilla Organisation, not forgetting the Bat Conservation Trust and Butterfly Conservation.

Although I support so many charities, I am actively involved with just a dozen or so, my particular favourites being The Brooke Hospital, SPANA (Society for the Protection of Animals Abroad), Born Free (slogan: keep wildlife in the wild), Animals Asia's Moon Bear Rescue Campaign in China and Vietnam, Tusk Trust and International Animal Rescue, which stopped the dancing bear trade in India and is now tackling the plight of orangutans in Indonesia. I am also heavily involved in many charities devoted to helping man's best friend, the dog, such as the Mayhew (our local shelter), All Dogs Matter – saving dogs on Death Row – Nowzad Dogs, working in Afghanistan, and Greyhounds in Need (of which my husband is Chair of Trustees), rescuing and rehoming these ex-hunters abandoned in Spain.

I suppose I would describe myself as an 'animal welfare activist' but am often quoted as an 'animal rights campaigner' which I definitely am NOT. I don't raid laboratories, releasing animals into the wild to destroy our native species, neither do I wear fatigues or Doc Martens. And I certainly do not wear face furniture.

But I am largely opposed to scientific and medical experimentation on laboratory animals and am a long term member of the 100- year old British Union for the Abolition of Vivisection, (BUAV) which campaigns to end all such animal experiments. Needless to say, perhaps, I am also dead against farming animals for their fur or feathers for humans to wear. The BUAV has pioneered many successful campaigns, including the banning of animal testing for cosmetics throughout the EU in 2003. But there is a long way to go before cruel testing is banned everywhere.

Another of my favourite charities is Compassion in World Farming, which campaigns to end cruelty to farm and food animals, including fish. The book 'Farmageddon', by CIWF's director Philip Lymbery and political journalist Isabel Oakeshott, describes modern, hideously cruel farming practices all over the world. CIWF believes that it is only by ceaseless campaigning that anything is ever done. As anthropologist Margaret Mead said, and this is quoted on the CIWF website, 'Never doubt that a small group of thoughtful, committed citizens can change the world. Indeed, it's the only thing that ever has.'

As I write, CIWF is campaigning to end long-distance transport of live animals, to end the suffering of pigs in Europe and to put a stop to the growing practice of mega-dairies where thousands of cows are confined for their entire lives on concrete in giant sheds and milked three times a day. Although these vast dairies are established purely for profit, the book 'Farmageddon' showed that many struggle to make a living. So often then, the cruelty is for no great gain.

After the factory farming of chickens and pigs, it seems that cows are next and that there is no end to man's inhumanity to the animal world. As time went on, the more charities I joined, the more I realized just how much animals needed our compassion and help. Whenever a war breaks out or there is a natural disaster such as an earthquake, floods or fire, my first thought is for the animals. When the nuclear reactor exploded in Japan, people fled, forced to leave their pets and livestock behind. There is also the plight of animals in the Philippines after the devastating floods there. I saw many, many appeals from charities to help the people but only one from an animal charity – the World Society for the Protection of Animals (WSPA). They are always the first to step in to help animals after a disaster, whether natural or man-made.

American psychologist Jeffrey Masson asked in his book 'Beasts', examining human attitudes towards animals: why is the human species so much more cruel and violent than any other on earth? Only humans, he went on to say, engage in mass killing, torture, slavery and imprisoning other species for food, hunting the uneatable for pleasure, killing out of vengeance and threatening the survival of other species and, finally, of all animal life on earth.

We kill, for food, 60 billion land animals a year, including one billion for leather and 50 million for their fur. Hunters in the US alone kill more than 100 million wild animals a year. We steal their eggs, milk, young calves and lambs.

On the other hand, Masson adds, human beings also exhibit the greatest altruism, caring and defending not just their own young but that of other species, often keeping them as pets.

Well said, Jeffrey! 'Beasts' not only enumerates the many cruel ways in which animals are exploited by humans, but also celebrates the great work undertaken by animal charities all over the world to alleviate the plight of suffering animals and improve their time on earth.

We certainly cannot look towards the church or religion to show us the way when it comes to animal welfare. The admonition in the bible that God has given humans dominion over the birds of the air and the beasts of the field is often taken to mean that we can treat them as cruelly as we like.

The Catholic Church seemingly does little to persuade its flock in Spain not to take part in the annual 'Fire Bull Festival' in Medinaceli, when flaming balls are stuck on to the horns of bulls, or the 'Running of the Bulls' in Pamploma where dozens of young bulls are released onto the streets and hundreds of young men, in order to prove how brave they are, taunt the bulls into chasing after them. When anybody gets gored, it is always the fault of these poor terrified animals.

Why, I have often wondered, are so many religions cruel to animals? At the end of 2013, The Times published an eye-watering picture of a man galloping a horse through 20-foot high flames, clutching a child in front of him. No, he wasn't escaping from a forest fire; the caption told us that this happened (and I quote) 'on the eve of the Feast of St Anthony, patron saint of animals, in the Spanish village of San Bartoleme de los Pinares in a 500-year old tradition that is believed to purify the animal.' Not only is this child abuse as well as animal abuse, but one minute the Vatican is telling us that animals don't have souls, and the next that they have to be purified. Bullfighting is still going on in Spain and goats are thrown from church towers at Catholic festivals while obese men sit astride donkeys until the donkeys drop from exhaustion. I could scream at this lunacy in the name of God.

One of the luckier donkeys saved from this barbaric event by The Donkey Sanctuary, was Blackie Star. This charity, founded by the late Elizabeth Svendsen, is based in Sidmouth, South Devon, and not only takes in sick, injured or abandoned donkeys in the UK but also works in Spain and Kenya. The Sanctuary brought Blackie Star back to Devon where he became a local hero. I went down to see him shortly after his arrival and he and Elizabeth posed for a picture for a short piece I wrote about his rescue for the now-defunct Young Telegraph magazine.

In 2012, while seeing friends in Sidmouth, my husband, Martin, and I went back to the Sanctuary where I asked about Blackie. He had arrived on 24 April 1987 and had six happy years there before dying on 25 May 1993.

The Jewish and Muslim faiths insist on food animals having their throats cut while fully conscious and with no pre-stunning. If you did that to your dog you would be prosecuted, and rightly so. Before refrigeration, this perhaps was necessary for health and hygiene reasons, but that is certainly not the case today. However, few governments ever dare grapple with this thorny issue, afraid of losing votes. Denmark was an exception in banning ritual slaughter in February 2014 but this new law immediately produced the question: what about the cruel treatment of pigs on Danish pig farms which lasts for the whole of their lives, not just in the few seconds before slaughter?

The Danish government – headed by a woman, Helle Thorning-Schmidt (married to Labour politician Neil Kinnock's son Stephen) – stated that animal welfare must take precedence over religion.

While I am emphatically not in favour of cruel pig farms in Denmark and wish the government would ban those as well, at least they are getting rid of one form of animal cruelty and one is better than none.

Since 2008, animals have been designated sentient beings. This happened thanks to a nine-year campaign by Compassion in World Farming, when an Article in the Lisbon Treaty stated that all EU countries must pay 'full regard' to the welfare of animals in agriculture and transport. The EU Slaughter Regulation states that food animals must be pre-stunned before slaughter, yet still gives exemption from stunning to Muslims and Jews, allowing them to continue with their centuries-old animal cruelty, in the name of 'ritual' slaughter. Does 'ritual' have to be a euphemism for 'cruel'?

On Thursday March 6, 2014, there were three pages in The Times about ritual slaughter, after John Blackwell, president-elect of the British Veterinary Association, spoke out against the practice, saying that it should be banned by law if Jews and Muslims voluntarily refused to adopt more humane methods of killing food animals. This happened in Denmark amid enormous outcry from

Jews and Muslims, who argued that the ban amounted to anti-Semitism. Jews and Muslims have even banded together to defend their beliefs and practices in this matter.

The Times report went on to say that more than 600,000 animals a year bleed to death in religious abattoirs in Britain alone (and what about other countries?). John Blackwell commented that while he respected religious beliefs, the Danish unilateral banning was done 'purely for animal welfare reasons, which is right.' Adding that animals felt immense pain during religious slaughter, he said: 'People say we are focusing on the last five or six seconds of an animal's life. It is five or six seconds too long.'

A Halal butcher quoted in the story said that a short prayer and a sharp knife dispatches animals quickly and cleanly. The butcher said he believed pre-stunning of animals before slaughter was 'sinful.' His meat is sold in shops across Birmingham with labels stating, 'non-stunned 100 per cent halal.'

Well! 100 per cent cruelty!

Britain is a democratic country and the law as it stands makes it illegal for animals to be killed without prior stunning but then there is a let-out clause for those whose religious beliefs state otherwise. People are perfectly entitled to campaign for a change in the law but NOT to simply opt out of it for religious or ritual reasons.

CIWF, naturally, is in favour of an outright ban on ritual slaughter. Stunning before slaughter makes an animal unconscious and unable to feel pain. This pronouncement is supported by scientific evidence which shows that cutting the throat of a non-stunned animal causes extreme pain and suffering.

If there is a God (and there are hundreds) why does He demand such suffering? Commenting on the issue, the website Atheism UK, says: 'The reason for ritual slaughter is based upon a false premise: that a god exists and commands meat to be slaughtered in a particular way.' Because of animal welfare concerns and the religious motive for

16

the slaughter, they oppose the practice of ritual slaughter and call for its end in the UK.

I don't believe in God but I do believe in DOG. And all other creatures ...

CHAPTER ONE

The 1930s

My love of animals – or at least my love of rescuing animals – must have started in the womb. When my mother and father married in 1926, they, like many couples in those days, got a dog before embarking on a human family. So a dog preceded me in my parents' affections.

The dog was a pedigree black and white cocker spaniel with beautifully pronounced markings. He looked rather like a badger, so they called him Brock.

Later, he developed eczema and in the days before antibiotics, the vet said the condition was incurable. Mistakenly thinking that the condition was contagious, my parents reluctantly decided to have him put down soon after I arrived on October 5 1930.

They took him to the local vet in Golders Green and the deed was done. Or so they thought.

Two years later, when my mother was pushing me in the pram around Golders Green, near to where we lived at the time, she saw a woman with a black and white cocker spaniel. He looked exactly like Brock and, curious, my mother asked the owner how long she'd had the dog. The answer was, since he was a puppy.

Not satisfied, my mother followed the woman to her home in Corringham Road, just nearby to Golders Green underground station. She did nothing but told my father that evening, who said he had dreamt Brock was still alive. The next day, they both went back to Golders Green and rang the doorbell of the house in Corringham Road. The same woman answered and there was Brock, his tail wagging.

My parents questioned her further about the dog – there was no doubt that it was Brock – and eventually, the woman confessed that her sister, who lived in Scotland, had bought the dog from the vet, who had miraculously cured him of eczema. As the original owner discovered she couldn't keep him, she gave him to her sister who lived right back from where he had come. As Brock had a good home my parents decided to leave him there and, apparently, he lived to a ripe old age.

Although I was not responsible for Brock's survival, I often think that my love of animals and hatred of any kind of animal cruelty, must have somehow been bred into me.

I, Angela Mary Vandervell, was born with green eyes and reddish hair. My parents, Kenneth and Molly Vandervell, nee Searl, had met through their love of sailing and were engaged for four years (no sex!) before they married. My father had always wanted to be a doctor but there was no money for training because his own father, Percy, had a secret 'other family' which we never discovered until decades later. When Percy and his brother Frank came out of the army after the first World War they set up a garage in Notting Hill and it seemed that my father had no choice but to go into the family business.

They then relocated to Belsize Park in North West London where they not only sold cars – a fast-growing business - but had the very first roadside petrol station going north out of London. Although my family on both sides was strictly urban, I was also born with a consuming passion, and compassion, for animals. This is in common with many kids, but while children often grow out of this passion, I never did.

In fact, over the years it became ever stronger. Some might call it an obsession but it is certainly my raison d'etre. Animals are at the bottom of the heap and I, along with many others, fight their corner every day.

As a small child, I would always try to pat, hug or kiss every passing dog and I was always falling out of my pram in my enthusiasm to embrace dogs in the street. I can just vaguely remember my mother pulling me away. The most popular breeds in those days were spaniels, Scotties, fox terriers and Airedales. There were also, of course, a lot of mongrels.

At the age of eight, while reading Black Beauty under the bedcovers by torchlight, I cried myself to sleep when Ginger collapsed and died of exhaustion between the shafts of his cart.

I've been crying for, and crying out for, animals ever since. One of my very first memories of animals being misused was when I was about seven or eight years old and my Aunt Miriam (known as Aunty Mimmy) went to a silver fox farm to choose a fox. Next time I saw her it was slung around her shoulders, with glass eyes and limp, dangling paws. I was horrified even then.

But it was not until the start of the Second World War – announced on 4th September, 1939, that I came directly into contact with animal cruelty. I was now nine years old and had a brother, Martin, four years my junior. We had been staying in Wroxham , Norfolk with Aunty Mimmy and her three children and their Nanny, when my mother and aunt suddenly became terrified that we were in the direct line of fire from bombs from Germany.

So one morning we were all bundled into a grey Riley 9, with my aunt driving, into the safety of Mid- Wales, where were found a farm to stay at.

Here I was, a city kid down on the farm, a bleak stone house called Pen y bont, in the little hamlet of Lidiart y Parc, in the county of Merioneth, now renamed Denbighshire. Life on that Welsh hillside was pretty traumatic for a nine –year old animal loving child from a London suburb, unused to the brutality of country living.

On our first morning, I was woken by the sound of animals squealing and bellowing and looking out of the window I could see the farmer and his lads throwing the male calves and pigs onto their backs, kneeing them in the groin and cutting out their testicles with a knife. There was no anaesthetic used of course. This was the first time in my life I had ever seen farm animals or seen for myself the way they were treated.

I nearly fainted at the sight, having no idea of course what being a farm animal meant. In common with other children of the era (and perhaps today) my only sight of farm animals had been in nursery picture books where cute sheep, pigs cows and hens happily grazed or pecked about in the yard under the watchful eye of a kindly farmer and his wife. There was no reality shown and certainly no cruelty to the animals.

This time, I did not see much more because two weeks later Aunty Mimmy panicked yet again, this time thinking that petrol was going to be rationed and we would be marooned out here. So we drove back to Wroxham and as a treat my cousin Francis (Fra) and myself were allowed to buy a couple of white mice each.

We were thrilled with our pets – the first I'd ever had – and took them back to the house in their cage. The next morning, we could not believe our eyes as Fra's were both dead. One of the mice had tried to eat the other and died with its mate stuck down its throat, head first - a macabre tableau, but this time humans could not be blamed.

The next trauma was that my mother and her sister had a terrible fight, the last in a lifetime of quarrels. So the following morning we were packed on to a train back to London, with my two mice in a cardboard box on the string luggage rack opposite us, where I could keep an eye on them.

An hour or so later I could see drops of yellow urine falling onto the black Homburg hat of the man sitting directly underneath my cardboard box. When I reached up to move the box, it was sopping wet and almost fell apart when we reached Paddington. Having got the mice safely home to our house they escaped, never to be seen again.

At the age of ten, I joined my very first animal charity, becoming a 'Busy Bee' of the junior arm of the PDSA – People's Dispensary for Sick Animals of the Poor, as it was then called.

The charity was founded in 1917 by animal welfare pioneer Maria Dickin, CBE, who was born in London in 1870, the daughter of a Free Church minister and the eldest of eight children. She was a bright, confident, independent-minded young woman who was never afraid of voicing her beliefs. Driven by the zeal of her spiritual faith and a determination to contribute to her family's meagre income, she decided to take a job. Women of her class were not expected to work in 1890s Britain but she ignored convention and opened a successful voice production studio.

At the age of 28, she married her first cousin, Arnold Dickin and, now a wife, was encouraged to give up her work to look after the couple's home near Hampstead Heath. Intelligent and witty, she possessed all the social graces of a society wife but giving up work left a huge gap in her life.

She launched herself into social work and, while visiting the poor in London's east end, was horrified not only by the dire poverty but also by the sight of animals silently suffering. In the streets were dogs and cats, raw with mange and often dragging broken limbs, scavenging scraps from gutters. Goats and rabbits were huddled sick and injured in people's tiny back yards while working animals fared no better; the horses and donkeys of costermongers and coal hawkers often crippled by heavy loads.

Tormented by the dreadful state of animal health in London, Maria Dickin made it her aim to bring lifesaving medicines to animals whose owners were unable to afford a private vet. She therefore opened her free 'dispensary' in a Whitechapel basement on Saturday 17th November 1917. So great was the demand that queues stretched down the road and she soon had to look for larger premises.

Within six years she had also designed and equipped her first horse-drawn clinic and subsequently a fleet of mobile dispensaries was established. By 1923 there were 16 PDSA dispensaries and also a motor caravan dispensary. But she didn't stop there. The PDSA Sanatorium in Ilford opened in 1928 as the first of its kind in Europe, specifically built for the large-scale treatment of sick and injured animals. It also acted as a training school for PDSA technical staff. By

1935, Maria had established five PDSA hospitals, 71 dispensaries and 11 motor caravan dispensaries. In 1937, a branch of the PDSA was opened in District Six, Cape Town, South Africa, a multiracial area originally made up of former slaves, immigrants and Malays brought to South Africa by the Dutch East India Company during its administration of the Cape. It was at the time a desperately poor area, housing the poor whites, blacks and coloureds. District Six later became famous – or notorious – during Apartheid, when it was declared a slum, and it is perhaps not surprising that the PDSA found a natural early home there.

The PDSA Busy Bees club, which I joined in 1940, was set up by Maria as a means of talking to young children about the charity's work and the need for good healthcare for their own pets. Her aim was 'Education, education, education' as Prime Minister Tony Blair said many years later.

As a Busy Bee, I held my first ever jumble sale in our back garden, selling bric-a-brac and anything that my mother's friends could be persuaded to give me. I made the grand total of four pounds – about £228 today – and that set me on the fundraising path I'm still treading some seven decades later.

By the time of her death in 1951, at the age of 81, Maria Dickin had received both the OBE and CBE in recognition of her work devoting her life to raising the status of animals in society. Not having the skill to treat animals herself, she did the next best thing and created the PDSA. Her reward was the sight of animals no longer in pain, and the thanks of grateful owners.

When Maria died, Enid Blyton, the children's author, agreed to take on the mantle, becoming the Queen Bee in April 1952 and holding the position until her own death in 1968. So popular was her reign as Queen Bee that over 20,000 new members joined in her first year alone. She encouraged Busy Bees to look after their animals and to raise funds for the PDSA. Her work continues today, and members of the children's club, now called Pet Protectors, are educated about pet care in a friendly and fun way.

It was perhaps hardly surprising that my first career choice was to be a vet, but first the War intervened and we were evacuated, properly this time, to a farm in Shillingford, Devon.

CHAPTER TWO

The 1940s.

The war was a bloody mess with men slaughtered, women and children bombed and millions sent to the gas chambers. But during the war I also became only too aware of the bloody mess which is the lot of animals, particularly farm animals.

My mother had brought us on the train from Paddington to this farm where a friend who had already fled the London bombs for the safety of nearby Shillingford, had found us rooms. The farm, called Dipford, belonged to Fred and May Webber, then in their mid-fifties, which seemed very old to me. The house itself was medieval, compared to what we had been used to in Hampstead Garden Suburb.

There was no electricity and our weekly bathwater was heated up by my mother in big black iron kettles on the open fire in the Webbers' kitchen. It didn't help that my mother was perpetually in tears. Not only was she unused to these primitive conditions but she sorely missed my father who was back in North London running the family motor business in Haverstock Hill, Belsize Park, servicing military vehicles.

Daily life on the farm soon brought home to me the reality of the casual brutality with which farm animals are treated. May Webber, the farmer's wife, kept twenty-seven ravenous farm cats which she never fed, believing they wouldn't catch rats and mice if they became 'fat cats.' But far from being fat, they were pitiful starving skeletal creatures.

Feeling sorry for them, I would beg, borrow or steal from the full buckets brought into the stone-flagged kitchen after the cows had been milked. I must have looked like the Pied Piper of Hamelin with a string of famished felines following me, meowing piteously. As I poured milk into the saucers I had smuggled out, the cats pounced on them, yowling and growling if another came within spitting distance.

There was also Nell, the poor black and white border Collie sheepdog, kept tied up in the manger in a dark, broken-down stable, fed on slops and never allowed inside the house. On the huge kitchen table, a freshly slaughtered pig would be unceremoniously butchered. Although the farm was full of animals, there was no sentimentality towards them and absolutely no kindness shown.

We had some fun, though. One evening Frank, the farmhand, asked if my brother and I would like to ride bareback on King and Prince, two whopping carthorses. Yes please, we said, never having sat on a horse before. Frank hauled us up onto the horses, their backs so wide we couldn't get our little legs round their enormous ribcages.

Frank opened the gate leading King, a chestnut with a black mane and Prince, a younger blond boy, into The Bier, a field with a deep slope which made it impossible to plough.

As Frank turned around to shut the gate, the horses suddenly bolted, their hooves thundering beneath us, manes and tails flying. We were two city kids, aged ten and six, clinging on for dear life. Blazing saddles! If only! But we didn't have any. Nor did we have any reins. And to think we had come all the way down here to Devon to escape death from a German bomb in London, only to narrowly escape being crushed to death by a heavy horse's hoof.

The Webbers employed a young maid of all work, Joan, whose job among other things was to feed the calves in the cowshed when they had been taken away from their mothers. She would put her hand into a bucket of milk so that they could suck her fingers; a poor substitute for the real thing. Joan earned 28 shillings a month – less than a shilling (10p) a day, although she did get a meagre bed and board thrown in.

I loved Joan because she loved animals but she caught ringworm from one of the calves and so my mother forbade us to go near her. But my brother and I got worms just the same and then we got scabies, which meant we had to have a bath every night instead of just once a week. This meant more heating up water in the big black kettles and then rubbing bright yellow greasy sulphur ointment onto our itching bodies.

But despite these parasitic infections, it was still Heaven being evacuated to a farm and surrounded by animals; animals which I could get to know and love – and rescue and help when I got the chance.

Shortly after arriving at Dipford we had a new house mate, a seventeen-year old farm hand named Ernest. He was angelic looking with blond curly hair and bright blue eyes. The only thing missing was a pair of wings.

He was one of the boys who, for one reason or another, could not be called up to join the Army and so were assigned work in factories or on farms. The Army wouldn't take Ernest because he was a bed-wetter. May Webber used to give him newspaper and straw to sleep on which had to be changed every morning, rather like an untrained puppy.

But Ernest was not as angelic as he looked. For one thing, he taught me to swear. When I used the word 'bugger' for the first time in front of my mother, she demanded to know where I'd heard it. Not realizing what it meant, I confessed that I'd heard it from Ernest. She was furious, rushing outside and, lifting up one of the carthorse's heavy padded collars kept on a fence, she threw it at Ernest. As he was so small and slight, it nearly knocked him out.

But worse was to come. While playing with my favourite cat, Blackie, in the yard, a police car arrived. Two policemen rang the bell and were invited in by May. Minutes later, Ernest was brought out by the policemen and driven away, never to be seen again.

I asked my mother what had happened and she said she would tell me when I was older. One day she did. Apparently, May Webber had gone into the cowshed and found Ernest standing on a bucket, fucking a cow. The cow probably never felt a thing but, classed as 'bestiality', it was a criminal offence.

Poor Ernest. He was sent to the slammer for an act which certainly couldn't be deemed animal cruelty while the Webbers, kindness itself to us townies, were brutal on a daily basis to their sheepdog and livestock alike.

My real nightmare, or more of a 'daymare' since it happened during daylight hours, was whenever the Webbers decided to kill a pig. The poor squealing creature would be dragged out of its sty by a rope tied to the ring in its nose. The rope was then thrown over a low wall next to the little garage where my mother kept her tiny blue and black Morris 8. Fred would pull the rope so tight that the pig would be forced to stand on its hind legs, lifting up its head. Then Fred would calmly slit the pig's throat, a bright red sticky river of blood spurting out and gushing down the lane.

I used to run up the lane during these times and bury myself in a big haystack, plugging my ears with my fingers until the squealing stopped and there was a deathly silence. One day, the rope broke and the pig, bleeding profusely, ran up the lane towards me and dropped dead at my feet.

Not long after one of the one of the pigs had been killed, my mother got a small parcel by post. Tearing off the string and brown paper, a box of chocolates was revealed. What a treat in wartime, as chocolates were rationed. She gently opened the lid and screamed. There, instead of chocolates, lay a curled up pig's tail, tied with a red satin bow, and a note saying, SEMPER FIDELIS - always faithful. Needless to say, the parcel wasn't from my father but Fred Webber's brother Frank, who lived on a neighbouring farm and had taken a shine to my mother.

I also dreaded Christmas because May would 'stick' the geese. There was a small shed opposite the kitchen door where she strung them up by their feet from a rafter, their wings flapping, and stuck a knife down their throats, blood pouring out of their gasping beaks until they flapped no more. It upset me for days. I never got used to the brutality of life down on the farm and still think about those dying geese every Christmas.

We were at Dipford in October 1940 and 1941 to see the pony fairs, where Exmoor ponies would be sold at the Bampton Pony Fair. This event was famous and is one of the oldest charter fairs in England. In 1258, Henry 111 granted Bampton its Royal Charter, allegedly because he wanted a share of the profits from this hugely successful event. In 2008, the Fair celebrated its 750th anniversary.

I of course attended this fair and cried my eyes out to see a lovely little foal going for a mere ten bob (50p) and my mother wouldn't bid. I begged her to buy it for me but of course she wouldn't. I often wonder what happened to that poor little long-legged bewildered baby. It probably ended up on a French dinner table, in a tin of dog food or, today, it could even be in a supermarket lasagne.

Because I wasn't allowed to have a horse of my own, my mother made a compromise and one summer, hired a pony called Dolly who came complete with a trap. The Webbers kindly allowed us to use one of their stables to house Dolly. It was wonderful to have this old-world form of transport, holding the reins while Dolly did a fast trot along the winding lanes of the Devon countryside. I was also able to saddle her up, riding off into the sunset Hollywood-style. And all this for eight shillings a week.

What about schooling? Many wartime evacuees have written of their experience of local schools, the latest being Terence Frisby of There's a Girl in my Soup fame, but my mother decided to have us privately tutored by two American sisters, the Misses Carrington. They were from Boston and owned a Bedlington Terrier, the first I had ever seen, called Fuzzy Wuzzy. Fuzzy looked more like a lamb than a dog.

Then my mother found a private school six miles away in the village of Clayhanger which had relocated there from Deal in Kent. For over a year my mother drove us there every morning in her little

Morris 8, after which it was decided we should become boarders. This enabled my mother to go back to London to be with my father. Although it was actually a girls' school, they took small boys up to the age of six, which meant that my brother could come too. The Matron of this school, Miss Ward, was the sister of osteopath Stephen Ward, the society fixer at the centre of the Profumo scandal. He committed suicide when charged with living off immoral earnings and his story was turned into a short-lived musical by Andrew Lloyd Webber (any relation to the farmers we were staying with?) in 2014.

I was very unhappy at this school as I had been nastily bullied by the other girls and when we got nits, my mother decided we would not be going back. Nits are quite middle-class now but in those days they were considered a disgrace and my mother was appalled. So my brother and myself were back in Hampstead Garden Suburb with V1 doodlebugs raining on us every night. My parents bought a Morrison Shelter – a huge steel table with removable steel mesh panels. It was rather like being in a giant cage and my brother and I were put to bed in it every night, with my parents diving in to join us whenever they heard the engine of a V1 cut out. The Morrison shelter was introduced in 1941 when night raids became frequent and was named after the Minister of Home Security, Herbert Morrison. It was an indoor shelter and a useful alternative to the better known Anderson Shelter.

The shelters came in kits which had to be bolted together in the home and although they were not designed to survive a direct hit from a bomb, could protect people from a nearby blast. Luckily, we never had to test it. Over half a million Morrison Shelters were made, and distributed free to households with combined incomes of £400 a year. Otherwise, they cost £7 – more than a week's wages for many people.

But now that I was back in London, permanently, I saved up my pocket money and bought two rabbits, Thumper, a grey Chinchilla and Hoppity, a pure white with black patches. I got a couple of guinea pigs too and not knowing how to determine their gender, put them in the same cage, with the result that I ended up with a menagerie of twenty-seven. I have always found guinea pigs to be sensuous little creatures, far more so than rabbits. When a male fancies a female, he purrs and wiggles his bottom about in front of his prospective mate as a sort of forerunner to twerking!

Hoppity escaped from her run one day and ventured out into the street. When I realised she had gone, I ran out to the front where I saw her on the pavement. Just as I bent down to pick her up, a passing dog got her first, grabbed her by the neck, shook hard and she was dead in a second. While I was standing there in disbelief and sobbing, a Jewish neighbour who was a furrier, walked by and asked if I'd like a pair of gloves made out of her. The very thought! That made me sob even more, and Hoppity was buried in our back garden with her fur coat firmly on.

Peace in Europe was declared on 7 May 1945, VE Day – and when the atomic bombs were dropped on Hiroshima and Nagasaki, Japan surrendered and the final peace was declared on 15 August 1945, VJ Day. I was on holiday in Cornwall with my parents and there was singing and dancing in the streets and waving Union Jacks.

So ended the war years. I was now fifteen and about to embark on a very different life. It was about this time that I was given a fox terrier puppy for a birthday present. I was thrilled to have my very own dog at long, long last. He was snowy white with a ginger patch over his right eye. I called him Toby and I absolutely adored him. However, unbeknown to us he suffered from epilepsy for which there were no drugs in those days and he had a fit while I was out walking him along the riverbank at my grandfather's bungalow up in the Fens.

My father called the vet who took him away and I never saw Toby again. Having waited so long for my own dog, he was suddenly gone and I was devastated. For as far back as I could remember, I had longed to be a vet, but as my father pointed out, it meant long years of studying so I set my sights lower, left school at 16 and reluctantly took a secretarial course, which my father had suggested.

It was of course, a standard rite of passage for girls in those days. You would learn shorthand and typing, get a job and a few years later, with any luck, marry the boss and give up work for ever. University and professional careers for girls were certainly not the norm in 1947 and few girls even stayed on to the sixth form at school.

My first job after completing the secretarial course was at Monsanto Chemicals in Victoria Street right above the station, where I worked for three years, all the time saving up to travel. Now, added to my love of animals, which was becoming stronger all the time, was a growing desire to travel. I did not realise at the time that the two would eventually combine so that I would travel all over the world supporting charities to rescue exotic wild animals as well as the domestic pets and farm animals at home.

Although I wanted to live abroad, I did not want it to be anywhere too 'foreign' so I started to look at countries coloured pink on the Atlas, somewhere where they spoke English. Madeleine, a colleague who had been evacuated to Canada during the war, suggested we both go there and we gave ourselves a year to save up the fare - £70. After the year was up, I had the £70 alright but she only had £4 because she had spent all her wages on cigarettes. So I looked for other options.

What to do? I did not want to embark on this early form of the 'gap year' entirely on my own. Then Daphne, a South African girl in the office, saved the day. She told me she was going home to Johannesburg and invited me to go with her. I accepted instantly, and intended to stay for a year. I had heard stories of black and white separation, but did not allow these rumours to stop me going. Once there of course I realised they were all too true.

CHAPTER THREE

The 1950s

My passage to South Africa was booked! On 10 January 1952, my parents took me down to Southampton to board The Warwick Castle, a ship of the Union Castle line. Daphne, my friend at the Monsanto Office, had already gone and had promised to meet me and find us somewhere to live by the time I arrived, after the two-weeks at sea. When we landed in Cape Town I took the famous Blue Train up to Joburg. Coming from still-austerity Britain, where many things were still rationed and food was scarce. I could not believe the wonderful three-course dinner on the train which cost just fifteen shillings (75p).

When I arrived in Joburg there was Daphne waiting to meet me as promised. She was half-Jewish and had rented us a room in an Orthodox Jewish household. Here was an instant double shock – a foreign country and a totally unfamiliar culture. On Friday nights, when the Sabbath began I would have to turn the lights on and off, and I became known as the 'shabbas goy.'

I was also asked to remove the gold crucifix I then wore round my neck. It had been given to me as a parting gift by a boyfriend and I had not seen anything wrong with it. Crucifixes were a popular form of jewellery in the 1950s and most Christian girls had one. But as I was a lodger in somebody else's house, of a different faith, I duly obliged and thought, not for the last time, what problems religion causes.

So my arrival in South Africa was a double culture shock; first lodging with in an orthodox Jewish household and secondly, becoming all too painfully aware of white supremacy in the country. Black and white friendships, never mind sexual relations, were a criminal offence, punishable by instant jail for both parties. Blacks were not allowed to sit on the same park benches as whites – I saw signs saying SLEGS VOOR BLANKES everywhere. Blacks were not allowed to go to beaches reserved for whites unless of course, they were nannies, looking after white children. There were also separate queues in the post offices for blacks and whites. However, although separated while buying a stamp or sitting in the park, black servants were allowed to come into your bedroom while you were still in bed to bring you early morning tea. I always thought that was far more intimate than queuing in the post office or sitting on a park bench.

Having qualified as a secretary in the UK, I found it easy to get jobs. English girls were prized as it was considered their training was superior. I had taken a six-month course at Bedford Square Secretarial College in 1947/8, considered one of the top colleges of the time.

My first job in Joburg was with the Shell Company in Rissik Street in the City Centre, where I stayed for eight months.

A few weeks after my arrival, on 6th February 1952, King George V1 died and a public holiday was announced as South Africa was still in the Commonwealth. A group of us crammed into a tiny Peugeot and drove through the night to Durban, where we lazed on the beach and rolled in the surf. This seemed like Paradise after the so-recently war-torn and still far from recovered Britain.

I soon had a boyfriend, Les, and a few weeks after we met, he proposed. I declined as I wanted to travel around South Africa and in any case, both being only twenty-one, were far too young for such commitment. After eight months on the Rand, I decided to move to Durban, exchanging the cool, dry climate of the mile-high city of Joburg for the hot and humid one down on the coast. There I got a job at Lever Brothers.

A friend of Les's, Larry, had also just moved there and so, both being new kids on the block, we used to hang around together, as 'just good friends'. One day Larry told me that Mike (Les's brother) and his friend, Roy, both of whom I knew, were sleeping rough on the beach. They'd left Joburg, hoping to find work in Cape Town but had failed and had arrived by boat in Durban, penniless. Larry and I went down to the Promenade to meet them.

There they were in brown double-breasted bird's-eye suits, ties and polished brown brogues, looking the smartest down-and-outs I'd ever seen. I felt sorry for them having no money and nowhere to sleep so I lent them the £70 I had put aside for my return fare to England.

The boys then went back up to Joburg, promising to pay me as soon as they had got jobs. I spent the next four months sweating it out in Durban not only because of the heat but also because of the stress of waiting for my money.

It never came, so I had no means of getting home. Instead, I got a job as a receptionist in the Mont-aux-Sources Hotel up in the Drakensberg Mountains in the Royal Natal National Park where the Royal Family had stayed on their tour of South Africa in 1947. I started work in January 1953, one year almost to the day after having left England.

For the first night, I was given the actual room in which the then Queen (the late Queen Mother) had slept in but was quickly transferred to a room the size of a box, with a corrugated iron roof. It was hot as hell in the day and freezing cold at night. The job itself was not what I expected, and the long hours combined with appalling accommodation led me to give in my notice after just two months.

During the time I worked in there I had got to know Bill Barnes, the Royal Park's Fisheries Officer, who offered me a lift to Cape Town where he was catching the ship to England to get married. He even helped me to find a boarding-house in the Rosebank suburb, which was rather grandly called Rosebank Hall Hotel. It was a complete dump but beggars can't be choosers and I was trying to scrape together my fare back home.

After eight months working in Cape Town at the Vacuum Oil Company as a secretary I saw a newspaper headline: EIGHTY GIRLS BESEIGE SHIPPING AGENT'S OFFICE IN ANSWER TO MORNING PAPER'S ADVERTISEMENT. Wow! Perhaps this was my lucky day. I tracked down the issue of the Cape Times where the story had appeared and found the ad: WANTED; GIRL AGED BETWEEN 18 AND 40 WITH BRITISH PASSPORT TO BE SIGNED ON AS STEWARDESS ON CARGO SHIP AND SIGNED OFF IN THE UK.

I most certainly wanted it and luckily the office of the shipping agent, Parry, Leon and Hayhoe, was in the very building in Loop Street where I worked. The following morning on my way up to the office my name was added to the list. I was number 81 – with no chance whatever, as it seemed.

But next day the agent rang to say I had been shortlisted to one of four, as the others did not have a British passport, and I was to be interviewed by the Master of MV 'La Cordillera' when she docked next day. I was offered the job and so asked my boss at the Vacuum Oil Company to let me go, which he did, and I was interviewed by both the Cape Times and the Cape Argus, the latter's headline saying, 'Angela says she would even scrub decks to get home.'

Little did I know how I could come to eat those very words and be quite literally scrubbing decks. But here I was, the world's great animal lover, about to leave South Africa where I had spent the last 22 months, without ever having been on a safari. With the Big Five – lion, leopard, elephant, buffalo and rhino – quite literally on the doorstep, I had not got close to a single one, and one of Africa's greatest treats is seeing wildlife in the wild.

But I simply never had the time or the money and the £70 I was owed still had not turned up.

At the time, BBC television was just preparing to air the very first wildlife programmes about Africa's animals, shot by Armand and Michaela Denis. This pair – Belgian-born Armand and his glamorous second wife Michaela – were to introduce the British public to animals they had never seen before, except in a zoo.

Their initial programme, *Filming Wild Animals*, was shown in 1954, followed by *Filming in Africa*, in 1955; then came Armand and

Michaela Denis, followed by *On Safari* and finally, *Safari to Asia*. Television viewers were gripped by these close shots of wild animals – in black and white of course - and also the fact that Michaela always had to apply lipstick as they got closer. I'm sure the animals appreciated the touch of glamour! Michaela also once said she could not possibly get into water with a crocodile until she had applied her eyebrow pencil.

Armand and Michaela became household names and their shows were much parodied but they introduced the viewing public to these magnificent animals that I had sadly missed during my time in South Africa. Although I have been on many safaris since, in those days safari holidays were rare indeed for British people.

On the day of my departure, a friend drove me to the docks with the two large suitcases I arrived with, plus the stuff I had accumulated, all wrapped up in a big Basuto blanket, a souvenir of a weekend in Swaziland with my boyfriend Les, his boss and the boss's wife. Having been signed on in the Merchant Service for my two-month trip back to the UK, I was now officially an Able Seaman. La Cordillera was a 6,000-ton cargo ship, one of two owned by the small line Buries Markes. I was to replace a girl left in Trinidad with suspected appendicitis and having no medical officer on board, she was shipped off to hospital.

Little did she know she had saved my bacon and little did I know that this young woman was Juanita Carberry, who was to play such a significant role in my later life and in particular, my work with animals. I was classed as a Stewardess, part of the all-female catering crew of nine and shared a cabin with a big jolly girl known as Bubbles. And my job entailed washing up for passengers and crew, making up bunks, polishing brass and scrubbing showers. After nearly two years being waited on hand and foot by black servants, this was certainly a come down.

One of the passengers was the late Cole Lesley, born Lesley Cole, sailing from Cape Town to Trinidad and onwards to Jamaica where he was to meet up with his boyfriend Noel Coward. Homosexuality was still illegal and Coward's liaisons were never publicly acknowledged. I made it back to Hampstead Garden Suburb in time for Christmas, and a new house, my parents having moved a couple of roads nearer to The Bishop's Avenue, the posh street in our neighbourhood. There was also a new dog; a black Labrador called Kim.

In those days it was relatively easy to get a job if you were a trained secretary and I first worked for a small camera company just off Shepherd Market in Mayfair, where many prostitutes plied their trade. Later I was taken on by the swish advertising agency J Walter Thompson in Berkeley Square, as secretary to an Account Director on the very high salary of £11 a week. I was mixing with a bunch of toffs who would appear in their country tweeds on Fridays, gun cases in hand. Needless to say, I didn't really fit in.

At the end of 1954, after I had been home for a year, my father told me he was taking on a young man who had just finished his National Service. Dad was now running Vandervell's Garage in Belsize Park and told me this new recruit was the son of an old school friend, Clive Humphery. Clive had got in touch with Dad as his son wanted to learn the ropes, having been Transport Officer of his unit in Germany. His name was Martin. When could I meet him, I asked?

Dad introduced us and it was love at first sight. On my 25th birthday and Martin's 26th (both born on 5th October), we had a party to celebrate our engagement. We got married the following April, a year after meeting, at Hampstead Parish Church and had our reception, appropriately enough, at The Fellows' Restaurant at London Zoo in Regent's Park. This was allowed as my father was a Fellow of the Royal Zoological Society. Guests had to come through the turnstiles where I thought they should have been handed a bag of monkey nuts.

We flew off to our honeymoon on the Costa Brava next morning, having spent our wedding night at the Grosvenor House

Hotel. Our honeymoon hotel was hardly romantic as our room had two single beds with mattresses filled with straw. We moved next day to a better hotel and met another honeymoon couple who persuaded us to go with them to Barcelona, to see a bullfight. I must have had a mental aberration to agree to go to such a thing. Utter madness. What on earth possessed me to go and watch and animal being stabbed to death?

We had seats in the 'sol y sombra' section and sat and waited. A big brass band struck up and in came the toreadors on horseback. That was bad enough as they were poor old nags covered with blood-soaked padding, probably because they had had their vocal chords cut, presumably so they couldn't cry out if they got gored by the bull. Then in came the bull. Totally bewildered, this handsome beast was goaded into taking a run at the horses, for which it got a spear driven deep into its shoulder blades. Blood spurted up into the air.

That was enough for me. I burst into tears and ran. On the way out, the gatekeeper saw that I was crying and asked, 'you no likey de bulls?' I screamed, 'I love the bulls, but no likey you!'

As our marriage got off to such a bad start, things could only get better. I stayed at JWT for two and a half years but always feeling a fish out of water, I gave in my notice and took the summer off. I've never had a 'proper' job since. People have often asked why Martin and I never had children. At first, I would say, they simply didn't arrive and after that, we preferred life with our freedom, our dogs and – increasingly – our animal charities. I think now that if we'd had children, I would never have been able to give so much time to animals all over the world.

We certainly could not envisage life without a dog. Our first was a dachshund, from a local breeder called Mrs. Bassett, and we called Humbert Humbert after the main character in *Lolita*, the highly controversial novel published in 1955. Humbert was only eight weeks old when we got him and I took him everywhere with me. We had him for six years, when he became paralysed and had to be put down.

Dachshunds often become paralysed because of their long sausage shape and short legs; it is a hazard for which every dachshund owner must be prepared.

CHAPTER FOUR

The 1960s

The next dog was also long-backed and short legged. A Basset Hound, called Harry. But he wasn't actually ours. While still grieving for little Humbert, I looked after Harry for a friend on a daily basis. Out walking him on Hampstead Heath one day with a girlfriend and her Old English sheepdog, we sat down on the grass near Parliament Hill and noticed another couple nearby who also had an Old English. It was Paul McCartney and his wife Linda. I jokingly called out to them 'Ours is a bitch, d'you want to mate yours with ours?' to which Paul replied in his inimitable Liverpudlian accent 'That'd be a laff, ours is called Martha!' Paul's song, Martha My Dear, is of course, a homage to that very dog.

On another occasion I met a woman, Grace, walking a Basset bitch called Buggerlugs and we decided to mate Harry and Buggerlugs as soon as Buggerlugs came into season. Grace brought her over but the two dogs, being virgins, could not get the hang of mating at all. In desperation I called Mrs Bassett, the dachshund breeder! She arrived with a tube of KY jelly, got hold of Harry's penis and shoved it into Buggerlugs. Nine weeks later, Buggerlugs gave birth to a litter of nine, born in Grace and Simon's country house in North Wales.

Grace invited us to come up for the weekend to see the pups. We got to the house but there was nobody at home. Instead, there was a hothouse full of cannabis plants. The pups were asleep in a basket, by themselves. I knew it was the Swinging sixties, but I was hardly prepared for what Simon was wearing – a black kaftan emblazoned with red cockerels and high heeled brown court shoes.

Simon, I learned, was an ex-journalist, gay and an alcoholic. Grace, also a journalist, told us she had married him because he needed a mother and she needed a child. When the puppies were weaned and up for grabs, an actor friend in Hampstead bought one but didn't look after her properly so I persuaded him to sell her to us. Cleo lived with us for twelve years until she, too, became paralysed. That was the end of Cleo and another loss. If these poor badly-designed long-backed dogs had another set of legs in the middle to support their weight, they might not end up like this, unable to walk. The breeders of pedigrees have a lot to answer for.

Grace, Simon and Buggerlugs all had a sad end. When they were driving to Chester to get photographs for their passports, they had a terrible car crash. They were both taken to hospital where Simon died. Grace's leg was broken and while she was recovering in hospital, a local farmer shot Buggerlugs, saying that she was worrying his sheep.

Meanwhile, my work with animal charities continued. After the PDSA, my next animal charity was the RSPCA. Having given up my job with JWT - and not looking for another – I decided to do some voluntary work for the Central London branch of the RSPCA, the biggest and best-known of all the animal charities. The Royal Society for the Prevention of Cruelty to Animals, possibly the earliest animal charity in the world, was founded in 1824 by a group of reformers led by Richard Martin MP, William Wilberforce, the anti-slavery campaigner and the Reverend Arthur Broome. In the late 1830s it set up a network of inspectors, for which it is still best known today.

The then Chairman of the Central London Branch of the Society was the wonderful Angela Cope who came to see me suggesting I did some fundraising, distributing collecting boxes around Hampstead and collecting in the street on World Animal Day, an annual event which started in Florence, Italy in 1931. The date October 4 was chosen as it is the Feast Day of St Francis of Assisi, the patron saint of animals. This is the day that very many animal charities combine to raise money, and is no longer a purely Christian event, as all faiths – and none – get together in a concerted attempt to raise money and awareness for suffering animals.

I would like to say something here about the psychology of collecting for charity, particularly when rattling a collection tin in the

High Street. Even in an affluent area like Hampstead, perhaps one in twenty people will put money in your tin. Strangely, those passers-by with a dog on a lead, almost never ever give. And then of course, when people know you are collecting for animals, they become indignant and ask: what about the children?

Whenever somebody helps animals or donates to an animal charity, there is always someone else who says they should be helping children when, in nine cases out of ten, these same people never do anything for children. I try to explain: 'why do you have to choose? It's possible to help both, you know.' Or even better, 'tell me which children's charity you support and I'll donate.' They never do.

When asked why I'm not collecting for children, I explain that Children's Day is a different day and that I hadn't seen them in the High Street collecting on Children's Day.

One year as I was rattling my tin, a man came up to me shouting that he hated dogs. 'Good,' I replied. 'Give me a fiver to have more dogs put down.' I went on to explain that strays had to be collected in a van with a driver, taken to a shelter, vaccinated and neutered, the owner traced and if they weren't claimed, rehomed or put down. Every injection, I told him, costs at least a fiver. He put his hand in his pocket, drew out his wallet, handed me a five pound note and smiled, 'That'll kill another one.'

When collecting for the National Canine Defence League, later known as Dogs Trust, (slogan: A DOG IS FOR LIFE, NOT JUST FOR CHRISTMAS) a man stood in front of me and said solemnly, 'A dog is for Christmas and if you eat it slowly, you can make it last until Boxing Day.' I laughed.

I laughed too, when a man put a pound in my tin and I explained that I couldn't put a sticker on his lapel because his jacket was suede and it would leave a mark. 'Stick it here,' he said, pointing to his right nipple. I did so. 'That was lovely,' he smiled. 'Now here's a pound for the other one.'

Such are the joys of collecting for animals. But nothing will ever stop me doing it although I have now given up street collections, concentrating on fundraising events at our house.

The reader may wonder why, as an animal lover, I have chosen to live all my life in Hampstead, rather than in the country. There are three reasons. I find the countryside cold and inconvenient and I live five minutes away from Hampstead Heath, which has 800 acres of heathland and woodland in the middle of the capital. While walking my various dogs, I have probably seen more wildlife in a single day than you might see in several years in the so-called countryside, which is almost impossible to enter and where so much wildlife has all but disappeared.

The Heath and the adjoining Kenwood Estate are one of London's great green lungs and I walk there every morning with my dog for 'my daily fix', as I call it. Away from the computer, telephone (I do carry a mobile for an emergency) and the real world, I relax in this green wonderland, walking there and back along a woodland pathway we call 'Birdsong Alley'. Here, magpies strut their stuff in their black and white DJs, ginger rabbits scuttle for cover, grey squirrels scramble up tree trunks while redbreasts, blue-tits, blackbirds and multi-coloured jays sing on the wing as they fly from branch to branch.

However, my very favourites live right at the top of the tree, twittering away. This flock of Granny Smith apple-green pink-ring-necked parakeets are the chattering classes of the bird world. Difficult to spot in summer because they blend in so perfectly with the foliage, in winter their brilliant green plumage stands out when they're silhouetted against the bare black branches. Although tree-huggers by nature when they do actually take flight, sometimes in formation, they look stunning. A flash of fluorescent green, their long tails give them the appearance of a squadron of Spitfires. 'The Green Arrows' we call them. Originally from the Indian Himalayas these exotic immigrants are now thriving here on leafy Hampstead Heath.

In 1966, an event happened which was to change the lives of all who were involved, including mine, although I did not become intimately connected for another two decades. This was the film Born Free, starring Virginia McKenna and her husband, Bill Travers. The 1960 book of the same name by Joy Adamson, which told the story of Elsa, the lioness, being rehabilitated into the wild by herself and her husband, game warden George Adamson, had already become an international bestseller.

In 1964, Bill Travers and Virginia McKenna, already well known film stars, travelled to Kenya to star in this wildlife film that was to change the world's attitude forever to lions. Bill and Virginia were profoundly affected by making this film, and their close contact with the lions made them understand that wild animals belong in the wild, and not in captivity. My own 'lion' story has many threads but it was nearly another thirty years before they all came together.

Looking back, it seems that my life has been a series of amazing coincidences and that nothing has happened in isolation. Even the way that I managed to become one of the cabin crew on the cargo ship home to England, by taking the place of somebody who had become ill, was later found to have close links with lions, Kenya, and my growing work with animals in other countries, not just our own domesticated pets.

Meanwhile, I had not forgotten about the £70 I had lent to Mike and Roy when they were sleeping rough on the beach in South Africa, money which had never been paid back. So when Martin and I went out there on holiday in 1969, I tracked down Les – who didn't recognize me in spite of having once proposed to me – and who now had a wife and teenage sons.

I told him about the money that Mike still owed me, reminding him that it was a loan and certainly not a gift. Les agreed and told me to contact Mike who was now a Director of the Anglo-American Corporation in Southern Rhodesia, now Zimbabwe. I wrote Mike a letter saying that I was in Johannesburg and had had my wallet stolen, thinking this might pull at his heart strings, if not his purse strings. He replied, saying he would give me the money the very next time he came down to Joburg, but by that time I would be back in England. I wrote again and then again, giving him the Nedbank account number of a South African friend. Mike replied saying he was living in a 'siege economy'. What a cheek! Even though he now had a big job, he couldn't transfer what had by now become a very small sum of money.

Then I had an idea. I wrote to the Chairman of the Anglo-American Corporation, who replied by return telling me I would shortly be hearing from Mike. Next day I got a telegram from Mike asking for that Nedbank account number which, of course, I had already given him several times. Living close to wild animals, he had obviously not learned never to mess with a party animal.

The money duly arrived in our South African friend's account, but with no interest whatever for the seventeen years he'd had the use of my money. I was so furious, I wrote back enclosing an anti-apartheid flyer somebody had handed me in Hampstead High Street, saying I had given the £70 to the anti-apartheid movement. Although very sympathetic to their cause, I had actually given the money to the RSPCA Hospital in Seven Sisters Road in North London. What a saga over what had become such a pittance!

CHAPTER FIVE

The 1970s.

This was the decade in which I became a journalist. I had never thought I would be able to write for publication, but once I got going, I found a wonderful platform to focus on animal stories. And of course my shorthand and typing background meant that I was able to interview people and take down their words verbatim and them type up my articles neatly and accurately. Thanks, Dad!

People are always interested to know how it can be possible to break into such a tough profession as journalism, especially when you are nearing 40 and have never spent time training on a newspaper or magazine. It is never easy, but it can be done, and this is how it happened for me.

A neighbour, Pat Miller, was Californian and when she left Hampstead to go home to North Hollywood, Los Angeles, she invited me to go and stay with her. At the time, America seemed to be where it was all happening. Airfares were astronomical in the 1970s but if you belonged to a club you could get a flight for a fraction of the price. I joined the Anglo-California club and got to Hollywood and back for a mere eighty quid – an offer I certainly could not refuse.

When I got home, I woke up in the middle of the night, dressed, sat at my typewriter and worked until dawn, writing a story about my Californian dream. When I had written it, I had no idea what to do with it and called a leading journalist friend, Barbara Griggs. Barbara was at the time fashion editor of the Daily Mail and later became an expert on herbalism, writing many books on the subject. I knew that she had many contacts in the business.

Barbara asked to have a look at it and kept it for two weeks. Worrying that my first attempt at journalism was complete rubbish, I plucked up courage and rang her. She told me she liked it and had sent it to her friend Shirley Lowe, deputy editor of Over21, a new and trendy monthly magazine of the time. Wonder of wonders, they bought it and it went into the July 1974 issue, as a double-page spread.

The story described my adventures in California, a place few Brits had visited in those days and, after it appeared, about twenty of my girlfriends kindly wrote in saying how much they had enjoyed it. Shirley Lowe said they had never had such a response to a travel article and immediately asked me to do more.

Beginner's luck? I now suddenly had a new profession, and had somehow to keep it up. My next double-page spread in Over21 was about a trip to India, where Grace had gone to live after Simon died, so as to be near her son Mark, who had taken an Indian name and was now known as Govinda.

Mark had followed the hippy trail through Afghanistan to India where he had become a sadhu (holy man), wearing saffron robes, carrying a begging bowl and living in a cave in Tamil Nadu. I couldn't believe it when Grace told me she had actually sent him a whole Stilton from Fortnum & Mason in Piccadilly. Must have looked incongruous in his begging bowl!

On a subsequent press trip for Over21, somebody suggested that I join the British Guild of Travel Writers, which I did in 1975. I remained a member for the next 36 years, going on press trips or fixing up trips of my own, selling stories on a freelance basis to many newspapers and magazines. It was a wonderful way of seeing the world and ruining it, as we used to joke.

On my very first trip to Kenya in 1972 I went to stay with a girlfriend from Hampstead who had gone out there with her teacher husband, soon trading him in for a coffee farmer in Thika. Little did I know that Kenya was to feature so prominently in my life. I well remember, on my first day there, they took me to Thika Falls where we had a picnic. What I didn't know at that time was that Thika Falls were to play an important role in a murder mystery which I was to become closely acquainted with. We also drove down to Amboseli

National Park for a couple of days and there I got my first taste of wild animals in the wild – a mini safari, at last!

Whenever I could, I focused on animal stories. These included spending a week with an RSPCA inspector in a deprived inner-city area of South London; going on safari to Kenya to get up close and personal with a hand-reared rhino; dropping down by helicopter onto the Canadian ice-floes to stroke seal pups; crying my eyes out in a horse hospital in Cairo; flying to China to the Moon Bear Sanctuary in Chengdu and driving down to Cornwall to see my erstwhile neighbour, a capuchin monkey. Joey had been incarcerated for a whole decade in the house directly opposite ours. If only I had known.

CHAPTER SIX

The 1980s

Everything now began to open out for me both in terms of travel and journalism, and my involvement with animal charities worldwide grew fast.

In the early 1980s, I saw an appeal in a newspaper for the Brooke Hospital for Animals in Cairo, formerly known as The Old War Horse Memorial Hospital. I sent a donation and have been an avid supporter ever since.

Dorothy Brooke's Hospital began life in 1934 and in 1984 I was invited to their 50th anniversary at a tea party to be held at the House of Commons. Of course, I immediately accepted. Richard Searight, grandson of the founder, and in those days Organising Secretary of the hospital's London committee, showed a video of working horses in Egypt and described how the charity was trying to alleviate their suffering by providing free veterinary treatment.

The guests wept. I asked if I could pass round the hat – hitting everybody in the wallet while they were still weeping seemed a good way of raising much-needed funds. I was told I most certainly could not do that in the House of Commons. However, I spied a wide-brimmed hat hooked onto a hat-stand at the entrance of the room where tea and cucumber sandwiches were being served. Snatching it while nobody was looking, I did a quick whip round. To my utter amazement, I collected three hundred pounds.

With this money, the Brooke took space in the Daily Telegraph and I wrote a short piece about the charity, which the DT accepted and ran. Five years later I was winging my way to Cairo to see for myself the work of this horse charity. Dorothy herself wrote of the Hospital on April 10, 1937: 'This hospital has fulfilled all my dreams.' She died in 1955, but if she were to visit the hospital today, I'm sure her comment would be the very same.

My own visit to the hospital, set in the dusty back streets of Cairo, was something of a pilgrimage. In 1989 I had read about it in the Daily Telegraph's Weekend magazine and also seen a programme, Vets of Cairo, on BBC- TV's 40 minutes. Over two million others did too. Richard Searight said, 'Within weeks we had quadrupled our membership and it certainly put us on the tourist map.'

Although there is an operating theatre, medical stores, maternity and isolation blocks, two ambulances, two mobile clinics and accommodation for up to 150 patients, this is no ordinary hospital.

Its patients are Cairo's draught animals; the horses, mules and donkeys which pull the local carts. Working in temperatures which sometimes reach well over 100F for long hours, they must subsist on meagre diets because the majority of their owners are poor and find great difficulty in feeding their families, let alone their animals.

Why then, is there a hospital for animals in a country where human health care is at a premium? The Brooke Hospital came about more by accident than design. At the end of the First World War, the British government sold off some 20,000 cavalry horses to buyers in the Middle East. Twelve years later, in 1930, Brigadier Geoffrey Brooke was posted to Cairo. His wife Dorothy, one of those intrepid upper middle-class British women, was appalled by the condition of the surviving horses she saw working in the streets.

She immediately raised awareness, as we would say today, of their plight, in this letter to The Morning Post, forerunner of The Daily Telegraph, in October 1931:

"There have been several references lately in the columns of The Morning Post as to the possibility of raising a memorial to horses killed in the War. May I make a suggestion? Out here, in Egypt, there are still many hundreds of old Army Horses sold of necessity at the cessation of the War. They are all over twenty years of age by now, and to say that the majority of them have fallen on hard times is to express it very mildly.

Those sold at the end of the war have sunk to a very low rate of value indeed: they are past 'good work' and the majority of them drag out wretched days of toil in the ownership of masters too poor to feed them – too inured to hardship themselves to appreciate, in the faintest degree, the sufferings of animals in their hands. These old horses were, many of them, born and bred in the green fields of England – how many years since they have seen a field, heard a stream of water, or a kind word in English? Many are blind – all are skeletons.

A fund is being raised to buy up these old horses. As most of them are the sole means of a precarious livelihood to their owners, adequate compensation must, of necessity, be given in each case. An animal out here, who would be considered far too old and decrepit to be worked in England, will have before him several years of ceaseless toil – and there are no Sundays or days of rest in this country. Many have been condemned and destroyed by the Society for the Prevention of Cruelty to Animals (not a branch of the RSPCA), but want of funds necessitates that all not totally unfit for work should be restored to their owners after treatment.

If those who truly love horses – who realise what it can mean to be very old, very hungry and thirsty, and very tired, in a country where hard, ceaseless work has to be done in great heat – will send contributions to help in giving a merciful end to our poor old war heroes, we shall be extremely grateful; and we venture to think that, in many ways, this may be as fitting (though unspectacular) part of a War Memorial as any other that could be devised."

This letter helped her to raise the equivalent of a million pounds. With this, she gradually bought up 5,000 cavalry horses still working in Egypt. Most of them were pitiful wrecks of the once-handsome 'Walers', so called because some had come from New South Wales in Australia, and their condition was such that they had to be destroyed. Those in unbearable pain were put down humanely at once and others were first given a week of creature comforts as the first and last holiday of their lives.

It was during the course of the War Horse campaign that Dorothy Brooke also discovered the plight of the native draught animals which were worked, regardless of age or injury, until they dropped. She turned her stables into a free veterinary clinic for the draught animals of the poor, and in 1934 founded the Old War Horse Memorial Hospital, or the Brooke as it is known today.

Since then The Brooke has helped millions of animals and also the owners who depend on their horses, mules or donkeys for their livelihoods. Animals are brought in voluntarily and are not discharged until fit for work. On leaving, they are re-shod, badly fitting harnesses are adjusted and owners are instructed in the proper care of their animals. Those who are too old, lame or injured to be treated are bought from their owners and given the now-traditional few days of comfort before being destroyed.

On my trip, we drove through the poor quarter of Cairo into Beyram el Tonsi (formerly called 'The Street of the English Lady' but renamed during the Suez crisis) to a welcome from Dr Salah who headed the hospital's team of five vets. As we walked around the spotlessly clean, fly-free loose boxes and operating theatre, a seven year old black stallion was brought in with 'knuckling' (ruptured foot tendons caused by too heavy a load). We watched as he was led out to one of the corrals where animals whinnied and brayed, nuzzled one another or lay stretched out on a bed of straw.

Each day a mobile clinic makes a tour of all the local markets, dispensing anti-tetanus injections and first aid for harness sores, and buying up old, emaciated or lame animals for destruction. We drove up into the Mokattam Hills to see the Zebbeline community of Coptic Christians who breed pigs and, during World War 1, supplied the British Army with bacon to go with their breakfast eggs. I can only describe this as hell on earth – rubbish piled high with women crouched down, picking through it, while snotty nosed children waved to us and the bloated bodies of dead dogs lay around in this wasteland of detritus. And that was before we got to the skeletal donkeys which pulled the rubbish carts up into the hills. There were no harnesses to take their weight, just old ropes tied around their scrawny necks which bit into their flesh with the weight of the overloaded carts.

We visited a market where I saw a man slit the throat of a goat. It looked up at me, lying on its back with a great gash across its throat, slowly bleeding to death. Dr Salah told me this wasn't officially allowed, but that a lot of terrible things went on in the world which aren't allowed. If a carter was trying to sell a horse, he would put on the brakes then whip the horse to show how strong it was by pulling on the reins, despite the wheels being locked. Dr Salah would shout at the owners, telling them they would damage their animals and then nobody would buy them but mostly, his words fell on deaf ears.

We flew south to Luxor, where tourists bargain with the carriage-drivers to be shown round the sights. At The Brooke Hospital clinic there, Dr Yousef explained: 'lameness is our worst problem, caused by carriage-drivers galloping their horses on hard roads, or more often, by bad farrier work. Old and ill-fitting shoes are often used but we're hoping soon to retrain a local farrier to Cairo standards.' Once a year, to encourage pride of ownership, The Brooke runs a competition in Luxor for the best carriage horse. Richard Searight, who flew out to present the prizes in those days said, 'this has become such a popular annual event that we are beginning to see a real improvement in the standard of the horses.'

Our last visit was further south still, to the town of Aswan, where a new clinic was opened in 1982. Here, Dr Gome holds a daily surgery, visits markets in the mobile clinic and attends to the 150 carriage horses in Edfu, as they wait patiently in the scorching sun for the tourist cruise-boats to arrive, disgorging their passengers into the carriages. And then their real work begins.

Through becoming a supporter of The Brooke, which celebrated its 80th anniversary in 2014, I heard about SPANA (Society for the Protection of Animals Abroad.) SPANA celebrated its 90th anniversary in 2013 with a wonderful party high up on Kensington Roof Gardens. What the Brooke is to working horses in Egypt, SPANA is to working donkeys in Algeria, although both charities have now expanded their work into other countries.

I soon became a dedicated supporter of SPANA and have held many fundraising events for this wonderful charity. Chief Executive Jeremy Hulme describes how it all began, and how it got going:

'In 1923, two redoubtable British woman, Kate Hosali and her daughter Nina, went to North Africa in search of winter sun. What they actually found was immense poverty among the people and immense suffering among the animals.

'Like so many other British women such as Maria Dickin of the PDSA and Dorothy Brooke, they felt that 'something must be done.' So, undaunted by the challenges and problems they would undoubtedly face, they founded SPANA. They were unusual women – brave, intelligent, well educated – and happy to fly in the face of convention. They had virtually no veterinary medicines, so they made up creams and balms in their kitchens. They had no antibiotics, no pain relievers no anaesthetics. Kate would disappear into the desert for weeks on end.

SPANA now works in some of the poorest countries in the world – Ethiopia, Mali, Mauritania, Morocco and the Middle East, providing free veterinary care for people at the bottom of the social scale, those who depend on animals for their everyday transport needs, and sometimes for their own survival. For so many of these people, their animals are everything – their food and transport, their present and their future. Without them they have nothing.'

In 2013 SPANA had to cease its operation is Syria but things were very different in 1988 when I joined a group of SPANA supporters for a tour of this country.

We had a date in the desert; breakfast of thick, sweet, black coffee with the Bedouin. We were on our way south from the town of Hamas heading back to Damascus and, as our coach turned off the tarmac road and climbed up on a stony hillside, young boys from the encampment ran down to greet us, their 'ghutta' – red and white headdresses – flying out behind them in the wind. Spring was a month late here in Syria and it was bitterly cold.

But this was no ordinary tourist trip; more a mission of mercy.

Our group of 20 were all supporters of SPANA, who arrived with their mobile clinic and before we were treated to coffee, the head vet, Dr Darem Tabba, had an important job to do – the very first anti-rabies vaccination of a dog. Here, dogs are most certainly not pets but working animals used to round up the sheep and goats. Never allowed inside the living tents, they lead a harsh life stuck out in the desert in all weathers and they are sometimes abandoned when the encampment ups sticks and moves on. The dogs then form packs which contract this deadly disease.

The owner of the dog, tall and handsome in black kaftan and flowing head dress, called it to heel. Crouching on the ground and cowering, the dog had its nose tied up with a bandage to stop it biting the vet. Injection over, it was fitted with a red collar to show that it had been vaccinated. The following year, when revaccinated, it would get a new blue collar, and so on. This programme was introduced not only to protect the dogs from rabies but also the Bedouin and their productive animals. Of course, it also protects the veterinary team, although they are routinely vaccinated themselves.

Until SPANA began working in Syria, the horses, donkeys and camels of the Bedouin, and the farmers, had absolutely no veterinary treatment. The Ministry of Agriculture's vets confined treatment to productive animals (cattle, sheep and goats) and the sick and injured other animals were just left to die.

Apart from seeing SPANA's vets at work in this primitive and barren land, we had also come to see two of the most spectacular historical sites in the Middle East – the ancient ruined cities of Palmyra and Petra. We would be seeing Petra when we went down to south into Jordan where we would also be able to see SPANA's work there. But first, up here in northern Syria, we paid a visit to Krak des Chevaliers (Castle of the Knights), perched on a mountaintop and the greatest of all the Middle Eastern crusader castles.

From the Fertile Crescent, a verdant valley where pomegranates ripen in the sunshine and cucumbers, green beans, lettuces and tomatoes grow in greenhouses, we climbed up a winding road from where we got our very first glimpse of this stunning fortress, standing on an imposing 650m summit, just a stone's throw from the Lebanese border. Although built 800 years ago to house a garrison of 400, it is still in pretty good shape, commanding views of the whole area, even down to the port of Tripoli in Lebanon and the lights of ships in the Mediterranean as well as the towns of Homs and Hamas.

Lunch was a particularly chilly affair up in the Knights of the Round Table restaurant as not only was there no heating whatever but a force 1 gale was blasting us with cold air through the ruined walls.

From Krak des Chevaliers, it was quite a culture shock to visit a camel farm with SPANA's team. A baby camel was bellowing in great discomfort because it was suffering from mange and had to be separated from its mother. When Dr Tabaa removed the sack covering its back, we all gasped in horror. It was completely bald. He gently rubbed it with a soothing ointment and then gave it an injection of an anti-parasitic drug, telling the owner he would be back next week and that it would be cured within a month.

We were then led into a yard where half a dozen or so adult camels were corralled, one lame with arthritis, which Dr Tabaa injected with cortisone. These gentle giants lowered their heads to take a closer look at us with their great big brown eyes, batting eyelids with eyelashes to die for, while their huge floppy lips moved from side to side and their feet did a soft shoe shuffle.

At yet another village, a woman walked tall along a dusty road balancing a pile of cartwheel-sized pitta bread on her head. Nearby, dirty water ran down the street into a putrid pool. This was our venue for morning surgery. A lame donkey with a stone embedded in its hoof had its foot inspected, while another had an eye infection treated. SPANA's team handed out leaflets which three Bedouin elders read intently. Translated into Arabic, they gave advice on how best to care for their most valuable tools, their working animals on which they depend for their livelihoods. If an animal cannot work, its owner cannot earn a living.

It was now time for yet another lunch, organised by SPANA's team in a Bedouin tent. Removing our shoes, as is customary, we sat cross-legged on big squashy cushions and were treated to a wonderful culinary surprise. Great bowls of steaming spiced lamb appeared accompanied by rice, diced tomatoes, cucumbers and onions, sheep's yogurt and fresh fruit. The lamb melted in the mouth. It was cooked not only with freshly ground spices but with almonds and truffles.

Syria is the truffle capital of the Middle East but, being a Muslim country, they are rooted out by dogs rather than pigs. Not many people know that, laughed Jeremy Hulme, our guide for the trip. He was right – not a single one of us knew that.

Whenever I could, I have gone to observe for myself the work that my 'abroad' charities are doing. One of my very favourite is The Born Free Foundation, which began life in 1984 and was founded by Virginia McKenna and her husband Bill Travers. The charity is now run by their son Will Travers.

Here, in Virginia's own words, is how the charity started. 'There is no doubt that for my husband Bill Travers and myself, life changed in 1964, when we sailed to Kenya to act in the film Born Free. The story of George and Joy Adamson, and the lioness Elsa had already been made famous by Joy's story and its sequels. It was an extraordinary story which told of the unique relationship between two people and a lioness – a lioness that eventually returned to the wild but always maintained her friendship with the Adamsons.

'We were just two actors. We knew we would be working with lions, but not much else! The two circus lionesses initially chosen were quite soon removed from any close contact work. We had realised, early on, that forming a genuine relationship with animals from that background was well nigh impossible. When during a contact session one of them tried unsuccessfully to get at Bill, the film crew realised they could not be used.

'It was George Adamson, the game warden, who became our mentor and lifetime friend. What we learned, we learned from him, particularly the necessity of seeing things from the animal's point of view.

'When filming was over, most of the beautiful and fascinating lions that had replaced the circus animals and who came to us from far and wide, were sold by the film company to safari parks and zoos. Both the Adamsons and ourselves were horrified. This act was, to us a kind of betrayal. But three of the lions – Ugas, Boy and Girl, were saved, and George moved up to the Kora Reserve in Kenya to begin what was to become the rest of his life's work.

'For Bill, too, this was life-changing. On our return to England he formed a film production company and made the first of his many wildlife documentaries. *The Lions are Free* was the story of George and his three lions, and it included a visit I made to Whipsnade Zoo where Mara and Little Elsa, the two lions we knew best, had been sent. I shall never forget the moment when they recognised my voice and came running up to the wire. No words can describe my feelings.

'Some of Bill's better known films were *The Queen's Garden* – a year in the life of the garden at Buckingham Palace, directed by James Hill, who had directed *Born Free*. *Bloody Ivory* was the story of ivory poaching in Tsavo National Park with David and Daphne Sheldrick. This was filmed by Simon Trevor. *The Lion at World's End* (see page 57) was the famous story of the lion cub bought at Harrods by two Australians, Anthony Bourke and John Rendall, and eventually returned to the wild by George Adamson. It was a story that would never have been told but for Bill's imagination, perseverance and persistence.

'But the film which, unknowingly at the time, became the catalyst for us was *An Elephant Called Slowly*, Pole Pole in Swahili. The story of the little two year old elephant calf captured from the wild in 1968 as a gift from the then Kenyan government to London zoo, has been told many times. She was with us for six weeks while we filmed and then the authorities said that we could buy her and give her to the The David Sheldrick Wildlife Trust. In 1977, Daphne Sheldrick founded the Trust in memory of her late husband David, founding warden of Tsavo East National Trust. The Sheldricks were pioneers in animal conservation, and the Trust concentrates on homing orphan elephants, rhinos and other such animals.

'But Pole Pole did not go to the Sheldrick Wildlife Trust as the authorities said that another calf would have to be captured in her place, for the zoo. So she left for London where she spent the rest of her life in a concrete elephant compound until her death in 1983.

'This led us to form our first little group Zoo Check, in 1984. Captivity was at the heart of our mission. Pole Pole's wasted life awakened us, as never before, to the unimaginable problems faced by wild animals in zoos and circuses. They are never able to express their wild instincts. Social animals are often kept solitarily and far-ranging animals confined to small enclosures. Birds are caged and unable to fly; bears display repetitive behaviour in their inadequate, sterile cages or pits and giraffes are kept in barren compounds with some token 'browse' and tied to a post. The list could go on and on...

'Our eldest son Will, who with his sister and brother had been with us in Kenya in 1964, started Zoo Check with us, and began to expand our work to include the challenges animals faced in the wild. Bill suggested we change our name to The Born Free Foundation, which we did in 1991.

'Bill spent the last two years of his life travelling around Europe visiting zoos, filming typical abnormal behaviour displayed by these captive animals. This proved, if proof were needed, that many animals cannot cope with these sad deprived lives. Sometimes they withdrew, sitting for hours on end in the same position. You may think this was in the bad old days. I fear not. Some zoos remain in a dark and sorry past. Elephants, the most family-minded animals, are forced to live alone; wolves pace; bears head-twist; birds pluck our their own feathers; dolphins live in small, concrete pools and do tricks to 'entertain' us. If only the audience understood, the people would weep, not scream with pleasure.

'It has always been a mystery to me that only comparatively recently has it been acknowledged that animals have feelings. Are fear, pleasure, depression, aggression, loyalty, only the preserve of humans? Anyone who has a dog or horse, who has read about the environment of the abattoir, who has seen cattle being herded onto trucks, or the expression on the faces of dogs in rescue centres will know that this is nonsense. So, in the wild, when we see elephants fleeing from poachers, calves standing by the bodies of their dead, mutilated mothers; the old solitary lion vulnerable to attack by hyena, the solitary buffalo facing the same fate from lions, we know that they mourn, that they feel fear.

'When dolphins are herded into caves and caught from the wild for use and exploitation in dolphinaria, existing in small, barren concrete pools, do they not feel fear, frustration and loneliness?

'I have never regretted for a single moment giving up being an actress. I know why I do what I do. And I care about it with undiminished passion.'

The Born Free Foundation, begun as a tiny little charity, has expanded into a global network, and is now an international resource working throughout the world to prevent individual wild animals suffering, and to protect threatened species throughout the world. In February 2014 , the now 82 year old Virginia McKenna spoke out about the dreadful trade of rhino poaching, saying that to crave ivory is to crave death, warning that the demand for illicit ivory threatens to make the elephant extinct.

Virginia was making a plea to Anglican and Catholic leaders to stop using ivory to make religious artefacts, and said`: 'Anyone who is in a position of influence, whether it's the church, politicians or leaders of society, you have to persuade all those people that seem to crave these little bits of carved teeth, that what they crave is a piece of death.

The United States, formerly the second largest ivory market in the world, announced a ban on domestic sales in February 2014, and McKenna said it was time for Britain to follow suit. She added, 'there are markets in London awash with ivory for sale. Whether or not it has sentimental value, a little piece of ivory is nothing compared to the sentimental value of an elephant's life.'

There are tons of things to carve, she pointed out, such as marble, which do not involve cruelty to animals. When Bill Travers filmed *An Elephant Called Slowly*, there were 35,000 elephants in Tsavo. In 2014, there were just 11,000. It is estimated that an elephant is poached in Africa every 15 minutes. McKenna said she feared that her descendants would never know the privilege of living in the wilderness that the Adamsons knew.

Note: George and Joy Adamson, whose work with lions gave Bill and Virginia the impetus to form the Born Free Foundation, themselves came to sad ends. Joy, born Friederike Victoria Gessner to Austrian parents in 1910, rose to international fame with her book of the same name published in 1960. The book remained on the bestseller lists for nearly a year. George Adamson was her third husband, and they later separated. Joy was found dead on 3 January 1980 at Shaba National Reserve in Kenya by her assistant Peter Morson. He initially thought she had been killed by a lion but it later transpired she had been murdered. George Adamson was murdered nine years later near his camp in Kora National Park while trying to save the life of a woman tourist being attacked by poachers.

While I was becoming ever more involved with the plight of animals abroad, I was still championing my charities nearer home, and decided to see for myself what the RSPCA, one of the first charities I supported, were up to these days.

In 1988 I went to Cruft's where I got chatting to Jan Eachus, an American born RSPCA inspector and I asked if I could spend a week with him on his rounds, seeing just what Inspectors have to deal with on a daily basis. It was one of the most harrowing weeks of my life and to think that these wonderful people do it every week of the year. I was thrilled when my story was accepted by the Weekend Telegraph and, on publication, I received a letter of congratulation from the then Chairman or, rather Chairperson, since it was a woman. Here's what it was like back then for an RSPCA Inspector.

Inspector Jan Eachus was all things to all men in his South London 'patch' – detective, policeman, photographer, social worker and vet. The common link was a love of animals.

Eachus trained guide-dogs and worked for the American Society for the Prevention of Cruelty to Animals in New York before coming to London with his English wife, since when he has been with the RSPCA..

As the RSPCA campaigns for funds to reinforce its Inspectorate, just 227-strong in England and Wales, Eachus said, 'We are totally over-worked and need more staff to cope with the growing demands for help.

'It's rather like going through a sewer in a glass-bottomed boat. In ten years I've barely dented the problem, with the RSPCA having to destroy some 80,000 animals a year.

'There should be a compulsory spaying and neutering programme, funded by a £10 annual licence fee. You could have an incentive scheme, with owners of spayed and neutered animals paying only £1.'

Eachus reported daily to the organisation's largest group communications centre in Lavender Hill, Battersea. There, five girls each take the 80 or so calls daily from the police or the Greater London public, these are then referred to the 24 London inspectors.

Most complaints are about dogs and cats but the day I was there one came from a woman whose child was upset at seeing live goldfish being fed to a crocodile in a wildlife park.

I set out with him early one morning to find out just what he might encounter in a typical day's round in a rough inner-city area.

Our first call was to a Victorian terrace, to see the owner of a small mongrel, ironically called Rambo, which had been beaten and kicked out into the garden without food or shelter. Called in by neighbours two days earlier, Eachus had rescued and taken it to a vet. He had also taped the owner's front door to find out whether he had returned in the meantime to feed the dog. He hadn't; the tape was intact.

Next was a visit to an old woman of 83, half blind, living in squalor and with no electricity. She had taken in four stray dogs, three cats and a rabbit. 'She would go without food herself rather than let her animals go hungry', said a visiting friend. However, one off the cats was in poor shape; Eachus offered to take it to the vet, and she agreed. As we left, Eachus told me he would alert Age Concern and the Environmental Health Officer.

When we arrived at the vet's, examination showed that the cat's jaw had been broken and it could neither groom itself nor eat. With the old woman's permission, it was put down.

While there we also took a look at Rambo, whose condition had deteriorated. Dehydrated, because of his internal injuries making it too painful to eat or drink, he had been put on a drip but would be destroyed if he didn't improve within 24 hours. He failed to respond.

Next came a routine call on a young man who had two dogs and had already been prosecuted for starving a third he had picked up in the street.

When he opened the door of his flat the stench was overpowering. The dogs were locked out on a tiny third-floor balcony covered in excrement. Eachus gave him a written warning. I asked him why he kept the dogs. 'I need them for company. My mum died and I don't have a girlfriend,' he answered. 'Judging by the state of your bedroom, I'm not surprised' laughed Eachus.

The next three calls involved Doberman dogs, one an emergency call on Eachus's two-way radio. No mobiles then. A man had removed his trousers in the middle of a shopping area and the police couldn't arrest him because his dog wouldn't let anyone near.

Our last call was to a ground-floor flat, to take photographs of an emaciated young dog chained up on a balcony, its only bedding a sheet of newspaper. It had been discovered by one of Eachus's colleagues.

Back at the RSPCA's headquarters, I asked chief Superintendent Richard Davies whether the law could be used successfully to protect pets. 'Prosecution is the final resort available to us and, to some degree, we feel that we have failed when we have to bring people before the courts', he said.

'The whole purpose of a uniformed inspectorate is for it to be seen and to act as a preventative influence – in exactly the same way as the police put 'bobbies' on the street. We raise some £13 million – but each year we're facing more calls for our help'.

So what's changed in the intervening twenty-five years? At Christmas 2013 the RSPCA took large amounts of space in the nationals stating that '100,000 dogs and puppies are abandoned or given up every year here in the UK'. There were 220,421 reports of abuse and a call to their cruelty line every 30 seconds. So much for us being a nation of animal lovers! The RSPCA now has an Animal Hero website: www.rspca.org.uk/animalhero. Anyone can be an Animal Hero by sending just £3!

Jan Eachus retired after 34 years with the RSPCA. The charity's total income for 2012 was £132.8 million and it now costs £32.7 million to run the Inspectorate (compared to just £5.9 in 1988), as well as £37.8 million for hospitals and animal centres, and a further £4.8 million on prosecutions and animal welfare. There are now 324 inspectors across England and Wales (compared to 37,000 police officers) up from 227 twenty-five years ago, with 31 working in London alone. It's a rotten but rewarding job and a lifeline for abused animals. Thank goodness three hundred and twenty four men and women are prepared to do it!

Although so many dogs and cats are treated cruelly – the work of the RSPCA and other charities devoted to domestic pets and animals goes on and on.

I cannot stress too strongly how therapeutic it is to have a dog, especially for singletons. There is always someone to come home to, someone who is always pleased to see you, no matter what!

It has been proved that stroking a pet lowers blood pressure while 'walkies' are not just good exercise for the dog, they are good exercise for us, too. I'm sure that the reason Martin and I are, at eighty-four and a half and eighty three and a half – the half matters at our age - in pretty good shape is partly down to walking our dogs, first Humbert, then Cleo, then Fancy, then Lunacy (Lucy for short), latterly Harry and now Percy. Walking the dog is also a great way of making new friends.

At the end of 2013, there was a newspaper story with the headline 'WANT TO MAKE THREE NEW FRIENDS? JUST BUY YOURSELF A DOG'. Owning a dog, apparently, can add three new chums to your social circle. Psychologist Dr. David Lewis stated: 'Dogs provide a perfect excuse for conversing with strangers. Many friendships, and even a few romances, only started because two owners stopped to chat about their pooches'. That's exactly how writer and TV presenter Ben Fogle met his wife Marina - while walking their black Labradors in Regents Park. Although Martin and I didn't actually meet through owning a dog, we have made a many new friends over the past five decades by walking our various dogs on Hampstead Heath. We always have a coffee up at the Kenwood Café, meeting up with old friends or, sometimes, making new ones. It's the best place in the world for networking. We like to call it petworking.

My last encounter of the 1980s with animals was in 1989, when I interacted with a seal on the Norfolk coast.

A group of us were facing out to sea and clapping but this was no ordinary launching. There we were, ankle-deep in thick, glutinous brown mud, standing on Seal Sand, a haul-out site in The Wash some eight miles off Hunstanton, returning the very first seal to the sea this season.

Swaddled in a blanket, the seal was gently lifted on to a stretcher out of the Tornado rigid-inflatable boat, carried up the mud-bank, laid out on the sand and unwrapped. Blinking in the bright sunlight, it took one look at us, turned swiftly around and with the flick of its flippers propelled itself back down the mud-bank and into the sea, sliding silently into the water and out of sight.

Just one week before, Alan Knight, a director of the British Divers Marine Life Rescue, and his fellow divers (an architect, a plumber and a TV researcher) had picked up this sick two-year-old male albino here on Seal Sand. 'If you can catch them' said Alan, 'they're ill'.

'When we came ashore here last Saturday' said Liz Varney, field-co-ordinator of the BDMLR, 'we all thought it was dead. I took another look at it and noticed its nostrils twitching and shouted to the others that it was alive and kicking'. Kicking it most certainly was. It took a team of six to roll it on to a stretcher and lift it in to the boat. Back in Hunstanton it was driven out to the RSPCA's Seal Assessment Unit in nearby Docking. The unit was set up the previous year, 1988, to treat seals suffering from the mystery virus which had reduced numbers in the colonies around The Wash from some 6,000 to a mere 300. Established jointly by the RSPCA and Greenpeace, it was housed in an old bus garage which had been lent by the local council.

With tender loving care at the unit from veterinary nurse, Jo Mangan, and seal handler, Doug Walker, the seal had responded quickly to treatment. Like all albinos, it was particularly susceptible to eye infections and, when found, its eyes were swollen shut. After being treated with antibiotics, it was wormed (lung worm is rampant among seals), its blood tested for the virus (negative) and vaccinated.

Freelance television researcher Liz Varney gave up her job for the summer and took up diving because she was interested in marine conservation, particularly rescuing stricken seals. A dedicated animal lover, Liz runs 'Catastrophies, a rescue centre for cats at her home in Kent.

She said: 'When I started coming out to the sand banks in The Wash last year, when the epidemic was at its height, I thought there must be something we divers could do. There was. We found we could bring in sick seals and take them to the unit in Docking'.

The work is likely to be permanent. 'Even if the virus is eventually wiped out and the seals build up an immunity, there's still a need for us to carry on', Liz told me. 'Every year pups are abandoned by their mothers, seals get sick with lung work or pneumonia, are injured by power-boat blades and fishing nets, become dehydrated, emaciated or covered in oil and get attacked by dogs and seagulls.

BDMLR was founded in January 1989 in response to the well-publicised plight of Britain's seals. Twelve British Sub-Aqua Clubs banded together to patrol the country's coastlines, rescuing stricken seals and transporting them not only to the Seal Assessment Unit in Docking but to the Orkney Seal Rescue Centre, too.

Concerned at first with the seal crisis, it soon became apparent that a much wider issue was at stake – that the welfare of all marine wildlife in British waters was in danger and that there was no properly funded organisation to help.

Ray Gravener, the then national director of BDMLR, had taken a sabbatical from his own electrical business to work full-time on the rescue fund while other divers, such as Alan Knight and Liz Varney, gave up weekends, holidays and even jobs to save our seals.

Although dogs make wonderful companions, it is not always such an easy matter to own one. Towards the end of the 1980s, we got a rescue dog from the Animal Welfare Trust – a mongrel resembling a miniature Alsatian, or German Shepherd Dog as I had learned to call them from my week with Jan Eachus.

We called her Fancy. She was adorable and when greeting us, after a prolonged separation such as a holiday, would take a running jump up into my arms. Every morning at breakfast while Martin was biting into his apple-a-day-to-keep-the-doctor-away, Fancy would walk up the wooden staircase directly behind the kitchen table, from which she had a vantage point, and wait. On the count of bite number four she would lean forward ready to be given the core. Whoever heard of carnivores crazy for apple cores!

I loved her to bits. She was the perfect pooch. No bad habits. Then one summer's afternoon going on to the Heath, we crossed East Heath Road, a race-track, and I let her off the lead once safely there. She disappeared and I thought she'd gone ahead and was hidden in the long grass so I ran ahead calling her. I happened to glance backwards and there in the middle of East Heath Road lay my dog. Dead. She'd gone back to get a bit of bread she'd seen on the way over. I was hysterical. I shouted at drivers pleading with them to stop. One man leant out of the window, laughing 'It's dead, dear', putting his foot on the accelerator and driving off.

At last a woman stopped and helped me get her limp body into her car, kindly driving me to the vet who confirmed that Fancy had, of course, gone long walkies. I left her there to be cremated and mourned her for the next six months.

When I rang the Animal Welfare Trust again, asking for a small dog, they suggested a fourteen-month-old Lakeland Terrier bitch looking for a home. And I didn't even have to drive out to their kennels because Lucy actually lived in Hampstead, just down the road. Her owner had died and his wife couldn't cope because she wouldn't stop licking their grandfather clock.

We went for an interview and there was the grandfather clock, stripped bare of its polish. We said that wasn't a problem because we didn't have a grandfather clock and took her home with us. However, Lucy wasn't about to give up the habit of a lifetime and began licking our skirting-boards, our doors and our cupboard drawers. She did it when stressed which was when we were going out or friends were coming in – she licked and licked until her tongue was sore and our furniture sticky with her saliva.

Our vet suggested we sought help from a certain Dr. Roger Mugford, a qualified animal behaviourist, who had recently returned home from America to set up practice here. On his first visit here he laughingly introduced himself as 'The dotty-dog doctor – not the dotty dog-doctor'! He called Lucy, Lunacy, and before we knew it we were on Breakfast TV being interviewed by Anna Ford who wanted to know if Lucy would lick her. Roger explained that her licking wasn't a sign of affection but a sign of stress and was confined to licking objects rather than people'.

He never did cure her and to this day whenever we meet at animal welfare functions, he laughingly reminds me that Lunacy was his biggest failure.

We then tried another animal behaviourist who suggested we put masking tape on our skirting boards, doors and drawers and made a paste out of olive oil and chili powder. 'That'll cure her in no time' he assured us. Having done as he suggested, we let Lucy loose. She ran around the bedroom licking off the paste without batting an eyelid.

We made the paste stronger. Lick, lick, lick. She never did stop until just before we had her put down aged fourteen. Friends said we should have been awarded a medal for putting up with her for all that time - from fourteen months to fourteen years. The inside of my wardrobe door still bears the stains from her saliva. I never washed it off, keeping it as a souvenir of the dear departed Lunacy!

But that wasn't her only bad habit. She was jealous of me getting anywhere near Martin. She would sit between us on the sofa watching television and if I got too close to her master, growl and give me a nip. One night we were going out to dinner and she was lying on a chair in the lounge. Martin tried to tip her off, telling her to go to her basket, but she ignored him. When he put his hand out to turf her off she sank her teeth into his wrist. Instead of heading up to the restaurant, it was down to The Royal Free Hospital for a tetanus jab!

One night she started barking downstairs in the kitchen and I couldn't stop her. Afraid she would wake up the neighbours, the only solution was to take up to our bed where she spent the last two years of her life. She slept at the bottom of the bed between our feet but if she felt my toes getting too close to Martin's she would bite me. We have a hole in the duvet cover to this day .

Seven years went by after Lunacy's demise before we could face getting another dog.

CHAPTER SEVEN

The 1990s

During the 1990s, my work with animal charities and my travels to see the conditions of abused animals for myself, expanded still further, kicking off with a safari to Zimbabwe where we had an encounter with an animal which was far from abused. Quite the opposite, he was positively pampered.

While lounging around the pool at Hwange Safari Lodge in the north-west corner of Zim (as it's known locally), I noticed a girl sporting a T-shirt emblazoned with the legend I SLEPT WITH ERIC. Underneath was a picture of a pig lying between the sheets and the words HE'S A PIG IN BED. I had to find out more. Nearby, so this girl told me, was a tented camp where not only could you view game from the back of a horse, but you could also sleep with a pig called Eric. Who could ask for more?

Next day we were on our way to the camp on the edge of Hwange National Park – the country's largest park, about the size of Northern Ireland. The five double tents were far more comfortable than I'd imagined; set on a permanent base, sheltered by a thatched roof and protected by a surrounding wicket fence, each had its own running hot and cold water and flush loo. So this was roughing it!

I sank back into the leather chair in the open-fronted lounge-cum-dining room while Ian, one of the two guys running the camp, poured me a drink and described the daily itinerary and the game we were likely to see. Morning and evening rides were available (each one lasting about two hours), picnic lunches were taken into the park by vehicle and dinner was served in the adjoining barbecue area.

Enter Eric. It was love at first sight. The size of an ordinary British farmyard porker – but covered in long blond bristles – he was, in fact, a bush pig and a wild animal at that. I gave him a big hug. 'Scratch his belly,' laughed Ian, 'and he'll roll over'. Within seconds was flat on his back, legs in the air.

Found as an orphan by a hunter, he was taken to Sikumi Tree Lodge where he promptly attached himself to one of the girls working there whose boyfriend was called Eric. At night grunting noises could be heard coming from her room and, since nobody knew whether they came from the boyfriend or the piglet, it was decided to name the piglet Eric, too. Should guests ask questions they could be told, quite truthfully, that Eric grunted in his sleep.

However, when Eric the piglet grew up he became too much of a handful at Sikumi and another home had to be found for him. Ian and his partner, Paul, came to the rescue and bundled him into a sack for the 15-mile drive to the camp. Eric didn't think much of that and ran off the moment they let him out and wasn't seen again for days. A that time the camp was only half built and Ian and Paul were sleeping on mattresses on the floor. Eric returned one night, lay down on the mattress next to Paul and went to sleep. Having got the taste for the soft life, he then learned how to unzip tent flaps and climb up on to the beds. One guest got a fright when she woke up one morning to find Eric stretched out on the bed next to hers.

Out in the stables Robert the groom was saddling up while Paul gave our group of seven a 15-minute talk on how to start, stop and turn the horse since it was the first time that most of us seven had ever been in the saddle. 'We always talk while out on a ride,' he told us, 'so that anything hidden in the bush will be aware of us and run off rather than attack us because it's been surprised.' So, having checked our stirrups; we were ready to go. Paul slung a rifle over his shoulder (there were always two armed guides on a ride, one going ahead to check for spoor), cupped his hands to his mouth and yelled 'ERIC!' The pig came running and off we set down a dusty track in single-file, with Eric trotting alongside. I was convinced he was a dog in hog's clothing.

We came to a stretch of open grassland and there before us, some 30 yards away, was a herd of grazing buffalo. These gigantic heavyweights are highly dangerous and can flatten you at the drop of a hat, but because they saw us as part of the animal on which we sat, they merely looked up and went on chewing. Later when we reached a small lake, surrounded by trees, the horses trotted along the water's edge while Eric lay down and took a mud bath.

On the way back, as the sun was turning the hush orange, we spotted a leopard crouching at the base of a tree. By the time we reached camp, the fire was lit and Eric, hog-tired, lay down, and fell asleep. For dinner there were kebabs and sausages. 'Pork sausages are Eric's favourite,' laughed Paul. 'He's even been known to beg for them!' Did I sleep with Eric? I'm not telling, but I did buy the T-shirt

My next dramatic encounter, though, and one which was to have profound consequences, wasn't with an animal but a very unusual human being – Juanita Carberry.

The story began for me (as it seemed – you will discover why later) when I went to an RSPCA meeting of the Central London Branch at Church House, Westminster, in the summer of 1993.

One of the Inspectors on the panel told us that they 'were having trouble with feral cats at Chatham Dockyard'. I jokingly remarked that 'since sailors are always drunk, you wouldn't expect them to look after their cats'.

The woman in front of me turned around and was clearly annoyed at my remark. 'Why did you say that?' she demanded. 'I was only being facetious and, as a matter of fact, was a sailor myself once'. 'What line?' 'As they only had two ships you'll probably never have heard of them - Buries Markes'. Thinking that would shut her up, she came back with a question. 'La Cordillera 1953 and did you get on in Cape Town?' Stunned, I meekly replied, 'yes'. 'Then you took my job' she said. 'I was the one left in Trinidad with appendicitis'. Here I was meeting the girl (now a 68-year-old woman) whom I'd replaced on that dreadful cargo-ship.

We walked to Westminster underground station together and she told me that, in fact, she hadn't had appendicitis but hated the

Captain, Roy Madison (whose name I shall never forget because The Madison was an American line-dance popular in the late fifties and sixties). 'I found him OK' I told her 'Ah! she said 'but he kept calling me bloody foreigner!' 'A bloody foreigner?' I cried in astonishment 'but you're frightfully British'. 'Yes, but I was born in Kenya and that made me a bloody foreigner to him' she replied. 'I'd signed a two-year contract and as jumping ship is an imprisonable offence I had no choice but to collapse on the dockside in Port-of-Spain and feign terrible stomach pains'. 'Good Heavens, so what happened then?' I asked. 'It worked', she laughed. 'They rushed me to hospital and took out my appendix'.

She gave me her card which I looked at after we split up to go home in opposite directions – she south to Chelsea and me north to Hampstead. The card read: 'JUANITA CARBERRY, gave her telephone number and the words Associate Director of WSPA (World Society for the Protection of Animals). This was yet another charity that I enthusiastically supported. So, apart from having both been stewardesses on 'La Cordillera', we also had two animal charities in common. Later I discovered that she, too, was a fervent atheist and I thought how ironic it was that we two non-believers should meet up at Church House, Westminster. Juanita had ticked all the right boxes, as far as I was concerned, but I wasn't prepared for what happened next.

When I got home, I excitedly showed Martin Juanita's card and told him of this extraordinary chance meeting. Had I not made that remark about 'sailors not looking after their cats because they were always drunk' the woman sitting in front of me would never have turned around and spoken to me. We could have been so near and yet so far from discovering our incredible connection. Martin looked at the card and said 'If her name is CARBERRY and she was born in Kenya, she must be Lord Carbery's daughter, part of that Happy Valley set!'

I rang her next day and asked 'Juanita, are you Lord Carbery's daughter?' 'I don't know' she replied. 'I have his name but I hope I don't have his genes!' I put the phone down. There was no answer to that! A few days later I mentioned it to a journalist friend over dinner. 'Have you read 'White Mischief' by James Fox?' he asked. 'No, but I've seen the film'. 'That doesn't count, you have to read the book. Juanita plays a big part because Lord Erroll's murderer confessed to her that he'd done it'. What next? I got the book and couldn't put it down.

Josslyn Hay, 22nd Earl of Erroll, married twice. First in 1923 to twice divorced Lady Idina Sackville (great grandmother of Frances Osborne, wife of George Osborne, the Coalition Chancellor of the Exchequer). They moved to Kenya in 1924 with the help of her money, becoming part of 'The Happy Valley' set, a group of elite colonial ex-pats, famous for their louche lifestyle, known as the three 'As' – alcohol, altitude and adultery – 'Are you married or do you live in Kenya?' being the catchphrase du jour. In 1930 Idina divorced Erroll because he was cheating her financially. He then remarried, his wife dying in 1939 of a heroin overdose. He joined the Kenya Regiment, at the beginning of World War 2, becoming a Captain and accepted the post of Military Secretary for East Africa in 1940.

That same year he met Lady Diana Delves Broughton, the bride and second wife of Sir Jock Delves Broughton. She hadn't been in the country long when she fell for the younger Joss Erroll. In January 1941 Sir Jock discovered his wife was having an affair with Erroll while they were out dining and dancing at the Muthaiga Club together with Erroll and June Carberry, Diana's new best friend.

June was the third wife of John Carberry and stepmother of Juanita, Juanita's actual mother, aviatrice Maia Carberry, having been killed in 1928 while piloting her own plane. Juanita was just three years old. John Carberry then married June Mosley two years later.

Born John Evans-Freke in Ireland, he succeeded as Lord Carbery at the age of six, emigrating to Kenya aged 21 in 1920, dropping the title and changing his name by deed poll to John Evans Carberry – with two 'rs'. He was a particularly uncaring and cruel father to Juanita, hardly ever speaking to her and referring to her as The Brat. He took her pet chickens up in his aeroplane and threw them overboard, and watched while her Governess beat her across the back with a bullwhip. That was the last straw, or rather the last whip, that broke the camel's back as well as Juanita's. She left, bleeding, on her horse, never to return, living for two years with her late mother's brother.

Many years later when she enlisted in the Women's Territorial Service (East Africa) she bumped into JC, as he was known, at the Norfolk Hotel in Nairobi. He asked if she thought he was cruel to her as a child, adding that he thought he was very generous to her since she wasn't his child, then telling her that her father was Maxwell Trench, his business partner.

After that fateful evening at The Muthaiga Club, on the morning of the 24th of January, 1941 Erroll was found shot through the head in his Buick at a cross-roads on the Nairobi/Ngong Road.

Jock was accused and Juanita, then a 15-year-old, was to have been called as a witness as she had been down to his house with June for lunch the very morning after the shooting. The following day he had driven up to the Carberry house, 'Seremai', in Nyeri, looking for his distraught wife, Diana, who had gone up there with June but they had gone out to lunch.

Juanita was home alone, save for the servants, when Jock arrived and so she invited him down to the stables to see her horse while waiting for the two women to return. It was then that Jock told Juanita not to be afraid but the police were following him. When she asked why he said that they thought he'd shot Erroll. 'Did you?' she asked excitedly, to which he replied 'Yes'. And he went on to tell her that on the way up to Seramai, he noticed he was being followed by the police so he got out at Thika Falls and, pretending to have a pee, threw the gun into the pool at the bottom. The very pool where three decades later, I was to have a picnic!

Although it was thought Juanita might well know a thing or two, she wasn't called as she was considered an unreliable witness. Jock was acquitted. Almost two years later he committed suicide at The Adelphi Hotel in Liverpool with a morphine injection. Nobody else was ever charged with killing Erroll and so it became a classic murder mystery.

James Fox went to interview Juanita in Mombasa some forty years later, armed with a list of questions for his forthcoming book, 'White Mischief', on the unsolved murder. 'There's no mystery' she cried. 'Jock did it – he told me himself the following day'. That was when he'd gone up to Nyeri looking for Diana.

My friendship with Juanita became ever more exciting. First, I actually got to meet the woman whose job I took on that cargo-ship, then she told me that she didn't have appendicitis, next I discovered she was Lord Carbery's daughter, then that she wasn't , and then that a murderer had confessed to her that he did it. What next? What next, indeed.

I became a Fellow of the Royal Geographical Society and used to invite Juanita as my guest to join the Society's Monday evening lectures. It was while sitting together one Monday waiting for the lecture to begin that I suggested Juanita wrote a book about her extraordinary life. She had kept a daily diary ever since she was a child and also had an amazing collection of photograph albums, every single picture captioned and all in perfect chronological order.

She took my advice and found a ghost writer, Nicola Tyrer, who did a superb job, bringing to life not only Juanita's harsh childhood but life in Kenya in that era, too, as well as her involvement in the Erroll murder. Since the murderer, Jock Delves Broughton, had actually confessed to her that he had done it, first revealed in James Fox's book 'White Mischief', making it a best seller, Juanita's own story of the event was depicted in her subsequent book 'Child of

Happy Valley', published in 1999. The cover has an iconic picture of a fourteen-year-old Juanita sitting on the ground, accompanied by her two pet cheetahs. I have now read it four or five times and I can truly say it is my most favourite book but then I'm probably biased as she was my most extraordinary friend.

In 2002 Professor Gunther von Hagens brought his 'BodyWorlds' exhibition to London to the Old Truman Brewery in Brick Lane. Juanita and I went to see this 'corpse art' as one of the critics called it. We both thought it wonderful – a cross between physiology and sculpture. In fact, Juanita was so taken with it that she signed up to be a 'body donor', her corpse to be plastinated by von Hagens when she died, laughingly claiming 'I've always loved travelling so why should I stop when I die'.

Two more coincidences with Juanita and friends of mine were discovered at a couple of our fundraising lunches. In the summer of 2003 we held a lunch for Born Free at which Juanita met Virginia McKenna for the very first time although, of course, she'd met Virginia's husband, actor Bill Travers, up at Kora while visiting her mate, George Adamson. Virginia's scenes as Joy Adamson were 'in the can' at the time, and she'd gone back to England but Bill was still there at Kora, playing George while filming 'Born Free'.

At a later lunch Juanita got talking to an old friend of mine, Bruce Bosher, who had been an engineer at de Havilland's. Both John and Maia Carberry learnt to fly at the de Havilland Flying School at Stag Lane in Hendon, North West London. Bruce was married to my very oldest friend, Pauline, whom I've known since I was four, our fathers having gone shooting together. On hearing about her mother being one of the first flyers in Kenya, he told Juanita that her father's aeroplane D.H. 51'Miss Kenya' was up at The Shuttleworth Museum at Old Warden in Bedfordshire.

In April 2005 we took Juanita up to Old Warden, not only to see her 'alleged' (as she always referred to Carberry) father's aeroplane but to actually sit in the cockpit which she'd never done in Kenya. She so enjoyed the visit that she decided to present to the museum the silver model of her mother's aeroplane (a de Havilland D.H.60 Moth) if she could get it back from Kenya. The model had been presented to Maia Carberry – with the citation – 'Presented by public subscription to that very gallant lady, Mrs. Maia Carberry, in recognition of her very fine flight between Mombasa and Nairobi accomplished under great difficulty and without special preparation. Her death shortly afterwards by an accident in the interests of aviation was deeply deplored by the whole community'.

The model was displayed at the entrance to the Maia Carberry Nursing Home and after its closure was hidden away on top of a cupboard, where a friend of Juanita's found it in 2005. Juanita got it back and Bruce and Pauline took her up to Old Warden in August 2006 for a formal presentation at a lunch of the model, along with a number of photographs and log books.

Miss Kenya was the third and last de Havilland D.H.51 built in 1925 specifically for John Carberry and was shipped out to Mombasa arriving on September 17, 1925. It was then taken up to their home at Nyeri by ox-cart and was first flown by JC on April 4, 1926, a month before Juanita was born. His longest record flight was from Nairobi to Kisumu and back in February 1927 to pick up the UK Director of Civil Aviation, Sir Sefton Brankner (later killed in the R101 Airship disaster). There isn't any record of Maia flying her, but she probably flew as a passenger.

Miss Kenya last flew pre-war in 1937, then being dismantled and stored in Nairobi. Post-war, the aircraft was restored to flying condition and was kept airworthy till July 1965 when it was air-freighted back to UK in an RAF Beverley. The airframe was stripped down and restored to airworthy condition by Hawker-Siddeley apprentices at Chester (ex de Havilland) and the engine was similarly restored by apprentices at Leavesden (where Bruce worked) and made its first post-restoration flight at Old Warden in March 1973.

Juanita and I became close friends from that first encounter at Church House until her death - at the age of 88, on the 27th of July 2013 - twenty years precisely. And how strange it was that I had taken her job on board 'La Cordillera' in 1953 and met her for the first time in 1993 – exactly forty years later. All the threes! We had become inextricably linked because of that coincidence, the first of many, during our two-decade long friendship.

She was a feisty friend, having very strong likes and dislikes, her pet likes being snakes and camels, milk and beer, her pet hates Catholicism, cucumber, cut-flowers, and cards (both birthday and Christmas), in that order.

In 2012 I bought a copy of Frances Osborne's new book 'The Bolter', a biography of her great-grandmother, Idina Sackville, who did a runner from five husbands, hence the title. One of her husband's was Lord Erroll and he and Idina became founder members of The Happy Valley set in Kenya. Not too surprisingly, Juanita knew Idina and was interested in meeting Frances, so I wrote to her suggesting a meeting with Juanita. In November 2012 the three of us had lunch at Brasserie Zedel when Juanita told Frances 'Although I was only fifteen at the time, I do remember that your grandmother had an extraordinarily long neck, probably the longest neck I've ever seen on a woman'. As far as men were concerned she seems to have had a brass neck!

In the spring of 2013 she went off to Kenya 'for the last time' she told me when she got back, adding 'I've been coughing up blood for the past three months – but it doesn't hurt'. She said she couldn't get an appointment because her doctor's practice was always so busy. By the time she did, was sent for a scan and got the results, she was in the final stages of lung cancer, having started smoking at the age of ten!

She was rushed off to the Chelsea and Westminster Hospital but when I arrived to see her, her bed was empty. She'd just been transferred to Trinity Hospice on Clapham Common where I went to see her twice. 'I don't know what I've done to deserve ending up here' she laughed when we arrived early one Sunday morning. Although she was sitting in a chair, eating her breakfast cereal, she said 'let's not beat about the bush, it's terminal'.

The second, and final, time I saw her there, I took with me my next-door neighbour, whom I'd recently discovered to be the sister of Errol Trzebinski (author of 'Erroll', her version of the murder of Lord Erroll) and long-time compatriot and friend of Juanita's. When I explained who Sophia was, Juanita's pithy comment was 'Why did you come now I'm dying. Why didn't you come when I was living?'

She also rebuked me when I showed her a big print-out I'd done of a photograph of her, me and John Rendall, taken the previous year at Chelsea Old Town Hall in the King's Road when he'd put on an exhibition of pictures of Christian the Lion, taken by his old friend, Derek Cattani.

John was one of the two Aussie hippies who'd bought Christian, the lion cub, from Harrods in 1969. As Juanita was not only blind in one eye by then and very frail, I held up the picture, explaining that it was of the two of us with John RenDALL. She raised herself up on to her elbows, admonishing me with the words 'Wrong Pronunciation. It's Rendle.'

Ticked off yet again! I kissed her hand and said 'Goodbye, old shipmate', her lower lip quivered as she gasped, 'Goodbye. Thank you for coming'. She lay there on that hot sunny afternoon, wearing a sleeveless cotton African-print dress and barefoot, I could see her wide range of tattoos. I know that today almost everyone sports an inking but back then when Juanita had hers done she was unique. In 1946 when she became one of a handful of women to join the Merchant Navy, she had her first tattoo, a small spider on the sole of her foot, later acquiring an African fish-eagle on her left shoulder above which was an elephant, and on her right shoulder an albatross. She once told me that she wanted to come back as one when she died.

She died three days later and, strangely it was John Rendall of Christian-the-lion-cub fame who rang to tell me 'she's gone'. Her body was flown out to Heidelburg where Gunther, who had become a friend and had visited her at the hospice, was waiting to receive her. I was hoping he'd have plastinated her by the time of her farewell party so that she'd be there on the doorstep to meet and greet us as an albatross. But it was not to be.

Diana Francis-Jones, the granddaughter of Maxwell Trench and therefore probably Juanita's niece, organised a wonderful party, 'Invitation to a Celebration of an Amazing Life – Juanita Carberry's Farewell' held at Carisbrooke Hall, The Victory Services Club, just off Marble Arch, two months to the day after Juanita's demise.

There was a magical display of photographs of her life with one hundred and eighty friends and relations turning up from the four corners of the earth – as far away as Kenya, Malawi and South Africa to nearer home, Germany, France, Scotland, Wiltshire, Chelsea and Hampstead. One of my favourite actors, Richard E. Grant, star of the cult movie 'Withnail and I', read a poem on the stage while some of Juanita's Kenyan wildlife pictures were projected on to the giant screen behind him.

Throughout the lunch we were looked after by Juanita's fellow FANY officers. As I said earlier, Juanita enlisted in the Women's Territorial Service (East Africa) on the 2ND of February, 1943, and served until the 8th of May, 1946, then going to sea with the Merchant Service – which is how we came to meet. When she came to live in England she rejoined the Women's Transport Service (FANY) in October 1991 at The Duke of York's Headquarters in the Kings Road, Chelsea, which has since moved to Rochester Road, Westminster. FANY stands for First Aid Nursing Yeomanry and the Corps is now known as FANY (PRVC) – Princess Royal Volunteer Corps, no longer being called The Women's Territorial Service.

There's just one more co-incidence in our friendship which must be mentioned. My husband's stepmother, Frances Humphery, joined the FANYs, as they were called, in 1976. Frances was Austrian and therefore spoke fluent German as well as French and Italian, and was appointed to run the Language Group. A year later she became Deputy Corps Commander, a post she held until her retirement in 1986, missing Juanita by four and a half years.

When Frances died she left a large portion of her estate to the FANYs, having recently changed her will just before her death, cutting Martin out which was unkind as he had visited her regularly, dealing with both her care home and financial matters for seven years. But that's life or, rather, that's death!

However, there were two guests at the lunch, long serving FANY officers, who were not only Juanita's close friends but friends of Martin's stepmother, Frances, too. And, of course, there were we two, with both the Juanita and the FANY connection.

I managed to find James Fox, author of 'White Mischief', whose name I'd seen on the guest-list and took him over to meet Virginia McKenna, who was sitting at our table. When I introduced James to Virginia he threw his arms around her, declaring 'I've been in love with you since I was sixteen'. I hope that made her day.

Juanita's last words to a friend, as she was fading away, were 'Be happy for me'. She'd been telling me for the past few years how hard she found battling with life alone, having little money, being partially sighted and with scoliosis that 'I've passed my sell-by date. I wish they'd put me down'. I jokingly told her to go to a vet instead of the doctor, a vet being more likely to oblige! Having no belief in the idea of a soul, an after-life, or anything so fanciful, like grief, I'll never forget her once saying to me 'I hate suffering in living creatures but when a human has died the body is no more important than that of a dead cat'!

I am now happy for Juanita that not only is her harsh and torrid life over but I'm pleased too, that she had such a happy and peaceful death. The care at Trinity Hospice was superb. Juanita was kept out of pain while being surrounded by all her many friends who beat a steady path to her bedroom door. On some afternoons there was a long queue.

There was an obituary of Juanita Carberry in every one of the nationals. In response to the one in The Times, I wrote a tribute to my fearless, feisty, infuriating and very funny friend who, because of her involvement with the murder of Lord Erroll, was famous, too. I shall miss her greatly.

This is perhaps the place to tell the story of Christian the lion cub which, although it did not affect me directly, impinged on the lives of many people who were significant in my life such as Virginia McKenna, Juanita Carberry and Bill Travers. And of course, it illustrates even further that animals are sentient creatures who remember, who can show affection and who return kindness.

When Juanita came to live in London in the early 1990s she bought a council flat in Chelsea, at the far end of the King's Road down in World's End, overlooking the Thames. This was primarily so that she could watch the shipping going back and forth. Sometimes she persuaded the skipper of a tug-boat to let her go along as crew for the day. Her love of ships was as strong as my hatred of them. Two months at sea on 'La Cordillera' was quite enough for me, thank you very much.

There was a big iron-grid over her front door and in spring, summer, autumn, and winter too, she had the actual door wide open, above which was written a greeting in Swahili ('Jambo' – 'hello') which she spoke fluently. In fact, it was actually her mother tongue, as having no mother she'd been brought up by the servants who all spoke Swahili. Although she constantly complained about the weather here being so cold here, she always walked about her flat barefoot and dressed as though she was still living in Africa. I went there a couple of times, but found it far too chilly ever to go again.

In about 2008, John Rendall went to look at the flat next-door to hers which was up for sale. On seeing 'Jambo' above her door, John greeted her in Swahili, having spent much time in Kenya. They got talking and discovered that they, too, had an incredible connection. George Adamson.

John Rendall subsequently told me that he and Ace Bourke, then in their early twenties, came to England in 1969, the natural route of Australians being Swinging London – famous for its music, fashion, politics and arts. They got a job, working in an antique pine furniture shop at World's End in the King's Road, heart of the Swinging Sixties. The shop, called Sophistocat, sold tables, wardrobes, chairs and desks. Whereas once pine furniture had stayed up in the attic, Manageress Jennifer Mary Taylor, brought it down to the dining rooms of Chelsea. John Lennon bought a pine table there. But John and Ace bought something far more exciting.

Having toured the Tower of London, their next London icon was the flagship department store of Harrods in Knightsbridge, then owned by House of Fraser. Today, although Harrods is currently having a £200 million makeover, ordered by its Quatari owners, it no longer has a zoo, But back then a friend had told John about the exotic animals being sold there.

John and Ace went up to the Second Floor to take a look for themselves and found two lion cubs for sale at 250 guineas each – a brother and sister. These sales were at the time perfectly legal but were outlawed by the Endangered Species Act of 1973. 'We were shocked', John told me, 'having been brought up in the bush in Australia I said something's got to be done about that'! And they certainly did do something about that. They bought the 35lb. male cub and called him Christian, after Christians being thrown to the lions in biblical times.

The two cubs had been born in a small zoo in Ilfracombe in North Devon and then acquired by Harrods. From his cage at this upmarket department store, Christian already had a paw on the social ladder, being taken to live in the appropriately named shop, Sophistocat, where he quickly became the most sophisticated cat on the King's Road.

Not only did he have his own two personal trainers, but his own personal photographer, too, and one with 'cat' in his name. Derek

Cattani lived just around the corner and was always snapping away as Christian marked out his territory in this urban jungle, from riding around Chelsea in John and Ace's open-topped Bentley and accompanying them for a 7/6d. lunch at The Casserole, to playing ball with them in the grounds of the nearby Moravian Church. This great big cuddly teddy bear with the amber eyes was also good for business, such celebrities as Ossie Clarke, Mia Farrow, George Lazenby, Diana Rigg and Mick Jagger, who rehearsed in the pub opposite, coming in to pay their respects to this supercat.

However, at eight months old, Christian had not only grown a mane, making him look quite fearsome but Chelsea's high-life of four meals a day, sometimes dining on fillet steak, had turned him into a fat cat – from 35 to 185lbs. John and Ace realised only too well that he couldn't go on living with them for much longer. Their gigantic pet was proving to be a gigantic problem.

While wondering what to do with Christian, and not wanting to send him to Longleat Safari Park or back to a zoo from whence he came, a chance encounter with actors Bill Travers and Virginia McKenna brought about the perfect solution. As luck would have it, they walked into the shop to buy a pine desk. Not too surprisingly, they were astonished to find a lion cub in this Chelsea basement, calmly lying there under a pine table as though it was an acacia tree in the African bush.

They were particularly fascinated because they had recently starred in the film 'Born Free'. The story of Joy and George Adamson who had hand-reared an orphan lion cub, called Elsa, and returned it to the wild, was about to repeat itself fifteen years later.

Elsa's two sisters went to Rotterdam Zoo in 1956, the very zoo where Christian's parents were kept, so there was a slim chance that Christian could be related to Elsa. No stud books were kept in those days whereas today zoos are gene banks for endangered species.

Bill asked the boys what they were going to do with their eight-month-old fast growing lion cub, snoozing under the table. Neither

John nor Ace had the foggiest and asked for advice. Bill immediately thought of George and suggested he might be able to help. George, fascinated by this new challenge, agreed to try.

While George was finding a suitable piece of land for this project and permits were being negotiated (not many lions have been taken from the UK into Kenya), and being too large and fearsome-looking to continue his walks on the wild side down the King's Road, John, Ace and Christian spent three months living in the countryside at Bill and Virginia's home, where they built a large enclosure for this now very big cat.

At last George wrote to say he'd found the ideal spot, a desolate piece of land called Kora, up in northern Kenya, where he set up 'Campi ya Simba' (Lion Camp). Christian had had weeks to get used to the specially built crate in which he was to spend fifteen hours for his flight into the wild with John and Ace going, too, to settle him in.

'I think George got quite a shock when he met us', said John, 'coming straight from the Kings Road with our long hair and in all our gear – flares from Granny Takes a Trip, whereas George sported nothing so trendy, his usual gear being an old bush hat, a pair of shorts and a pipe stuck in his mouth'.

A year later, in 1971, John and Ace went back to Kora where they were reunited with Christian. George called out to this now wild lion, and there he was with two young lionesses. When he saw the two boys, this handsome, fully grown beast came running, leaping up and putting his huge great paws around their necks, licking their faces and nuzzling their legs when he could, of course, just as easily have killed them. They say that elephants never forget but, apparently, neither do lions!

Bill Travers along with James Hill, Director of 'Born Free', decided to make a documentary of Christian's transformation from Chelsea cuddly pet to African wild beast which they called 'The Lion at World's End'. A video clip of Christian's reunion with John and Ace from the film was posted on YouTube in 2009, since when it has had over one hundred million hits with Christian becoming an ambassador for conservation. (Click on LION REUNION and other clips will pop up, too.)

Christian disappeared in 1973, not coming back to George because he didn't need to. He had been successfully rehabilitated. George heard him mating and there was never any account of him having been killed. The death of a 600lb. lion up at Kora would certainly have been reported, local lions never weighing more than 400lbs.

In 1972 Tony Fitzjohn, known as Fitz, a young rebel from the UK arrived out of the blue up at Kora and became George's assistant, staying with him till 1988, the year before he was murdered. In 1980 The George Adamson Wildlife Preservation Trust was founded by a group of George's friends and, following his murder, Tony Fitzjohn became the Field Director of the Trust which supports and runs education programmes and does work in Kora as well as in Tanzania, where it is reintroducing the endangered black rhino and the hunting dog.

In a recent TV documentary, 'A Lion Called Mugie', Doc Martin actor, Martin Clunes, travels to the newly rebuilt camp at Kora to interview Fitz who is trying to reintroduce endangered lions into the wild there. Sadly, Mugie, an orphaned cub which he was rearing was killed by hyenas while out on a daily walk. Fitz explained that there are now a mere 20,000 lions left in the wild, whereas hyenas are proliferating due to the number of game killed by poachers. They are now the fat cats of the bush and the natural balance of nature is completely out of kilter.

While both Chester Zoo and Tusk Trust sponsor the George Adamson Wildlife Preservation Trust, Bob Marshall Andrews QC, MP, is currently Chairman, Princess Michael of Kent is Patron and John Rendall a Trustee as well as my old colleague from the British Guild of Travel Writers, wildlife and Africa expert, Brian Jackman. Five years ago when returning from a safari in Tanzania, we were waiting at a tiny airstrip for four more passengers to arrive for the light-aircraft flight back to Dar es Salaam. When they arrived in their open-topped vehicle, there was Brian and his wife, Annabel.

John Rendall told me that 'When Christian went out to Kenya there were 300,000 lions in Africa. Today the West African lion is extinct with lions left in only six countries in Africa. The total is less than 20,000 with fewer than 2,000 in Kenya and 4,000 in captive ownership'.

'Loss is due to hunting, poaching and poisoning and with the exploding population (in 1960 in Kenya there were 8 million while today there are 40 million) dominating the traditional lion's hunting grounds, so they can graze their cattle, the lion is running out of space. If the top predator is safe and healthy all the other animals will be safe and healthy – healthy lions, healthy herbivores – which means you have plenty of grass and water and therefore everything else is healthy. If you lose your lions everything else is out of kilter'.

While Juanita was still living in Kenya, being an avid animal lover (she used to hate that description, saying 'it sounds as though you fuck ducks') it isn't too surprising that not only did she know George and Joy Adamson but George became one of her great mates and when he was murdered she was gutted.

So, here she was living in a council flat in World's End, Chelsea, and quite by chance, meeting up with John Rendall who was also a great mate of George's. Another coincidence.

In the autumn of 2012 Juanita told me that John Rendall and snapper Derek Cattani were having an exhibition of pictures of Christian which Derek had taken in the seventies, in aid of The George Adamson Wildlife Preservation Trust.

We went along together and I met John and Derek, buying one the iconic images of John and Ace, standing in the King's Road with John holding this great lump of a lion in his arms, sporting a fur coat similar to the one Christian is wearing. Today, John would be shot and quite rightly so! Derek took a picture of John, Juanita and me (the very one which I printed out and took to her in the Trinity Hospice when she ticked me off for mispronouncing John's surname) with my purchase on the wall behind us. They hang in our lounge today as a reminder of all those coincidental meetings between the three of us.

John was back in the news early in January 2014 because Harrods had announced that it was closing down its pet department, known as the Pet Kingdom, at the end of the month after almost a century of selling animals.

' I went there on the day it closed' John told me 'and spoke to many of the staff who told me that at least twice a day customers asked about Christian'. The original Harrods Zoo closed in 1976 but before it did, apart from Christian, an alligator was bought by writer and playwright Noel Coward and a baby elephant was sold to Ronald Reagan when he became governor of California in the 1970s'.

The final closure of the Pet Department was an excuse for the London Evening Standard to rehash the story about John and Ace buying a lion cub at Harrods and to reprint the famous picture of them in their open-topped Bentley in 1969, with a very cuddly looking Christian hanging out of the back.

Juanita taught me much about Africa's wildlife as well as about the colonial era in Kenya. Two years after we met, she rang to tell me to turn on the television quickly as there was a BBC programme about Lewa Downs in Kenya where a giraffe was browsing on the white bougainvillea in the garden of this cattle ranch, owned by David and Delia Craig.

Shortly afterwards there was a story in the BBC Wildlife Magazine about Anna Merz, an English woman who had founded the Lewa Wildlife Conservancy in Kenya, paying out of her own pocket for the erection of a gigantic electric-wire fence, encompassing the property, into which endangered rhino were relocated. While living at Lewa she had successfully hand-reared an orphaned baby rhino, Samia, and returned it to the wild. What a story!

This was in 1995 and I wrote to Anna explaining that I wanted to do a story about Samia, and could we come and stay with her for a couple of nights, offering a donation to the Conservancy in return for her time and hospitality. I was over the moon when she agreed.

To get the most mileage out of our trip, we decided to combine it with a visit to my adopted orphan elephant, Emily. Through the charity, Care for the Wild, Martin had given me a year's sponsorship for Emily as a Christmas present. She was being cared for at The David Sheldrick Wildife Trust just outside Nairobi. As I had a second cousin, Duncan Fraser, living in Karen in the actual house which once belonged to Karen Blixen, named after the 'Out of Africa' lady, I asked if we could come for a quick visit on our way up north. He was delighted to host us and to show us around. Here I was about to live my very own version of Gerald Durrell's bestseller 'My Family and Other Animals'.

Before leaving, Juanita had given me pictures and a description of the house she had designed and built in Karen, subsequently compulsorily purchased by a government minister. It had the most wonderful avenue of jacarandas which she had had planted. I couldn't wait to see it. But before I was able to mention this to my cousin on the way to his house from the airport, he said we had to stop off at a friend's home to deliver something. As we drove up that avenue of jacarandas, I couldn't believe my eyes. This very house was, in fact, Juanita's. Yet another coincidence in our saga.

While staying with Duncan and his wife, Jill, they kindly took us out to meet Emily. I'd had to wait almost a month before I could see, let alone touch, my Christmas present. Daphne Sheldrick, widow of the late David Sheldrick, who was founder Warden of Tsavo National Park, has been rearing and rehabilitating orphans of misfortune for most of her life. Emily was brought to her at a month old, abandoned by her mother after having fallen into a refuse pit. In the wild, elephants are dependent on their mother's milk for their first two years, and so Emily, fifteen months old, was still being bottle fed every four hours, drinking 36 pints a day of the special milk formula Daphne had developed. When she was older, she would gradually be reintroduced to the wild, joining the rehabilitation programme in Tsavo National Park, together with the other elephants.

We got there for feeding time at 11am. I've heard of pink elephants but I wasn't prepared for a red one. Perhaps she was still in her Christmas wrapping? In fact, she was red from the mud baths the keepers give them to protect their skin from sunburn. Sunscreen is also put on to their ears, which are particularly susceptible, and the youngest of the three then in the nursery was wearing a rug for extra protection. In the wild they stay underneath their mothers for shelter.

When I showed Emily the photograph of her that Care for the Wild had sent me, thinking that she might autograph it, she gripped hold of it with the tip of her trunk, wrenched it out of my hand and threw it on the ground. Emily was eventually taken to Tsavo where she has now given birth to her own calf.

It was then off to Wilson Airport and up to Nanyuki where Anna was to meet us. 'What Joy Adamson was to lions, Dian Fossey was to gorillas, and Jane Goodall is to chimpanzees, Anna Merz is to rhinos...' so wrote Desmond Morris in his foreword to her book 'Rhino at the Brink of Extinction'. How tragic that, almost three decades later, the problem has only got worse.

Despite her name, acquired on marriage to a Swiss husband, Anna Merz was a true Brit and, like so many of her fellow compatriots, had an overwhelming passion (or, rather, compassion) for animals all her life. She was one of those middle-class frontierswomen, fast becoming an endangered species like the rhino she'd been fighting to save in Kenya for the past two decades.

One of the very first things she said to me was 'the rhino needs a good Public Relations Officer', little knowing that almost two decades later, Prince William was to become that 'good Public Relations Officer' on behalf of this medieval creature. It has a low profile because it's the ugly duckling of the animal world. It isn't cuddly and it doesn't have big brown eyes. It has a tough, wrinkly hide and tiny eyes, added to which it has the reputation of being stupid, solitary and incredibly bad tempered.

'Rubbish!' snorted Anna – and who should know better? Not only had she been running the Ngare Sergoi Rhino Sanctuary for the past eleven years but she was one of the very few people ever to have reared a rhino calf from birth. That very calf, a black rhino called Samia was by now a completely wild animal, mixing with her own species and currently in calf, but still retaining an affectionate relationship with Anna, her adoptive mother.

On our very first morning out in the bush with Anna she scoured the landscape while driving the Land Rover, looking for that great grey beast. She knew roughly the area Samia inhabited and we hadn't gone more than a couple of miles from the house when she slammed on the brakes, raised her binoculars and turned off the engine. Taking a paper sack of horse-nuts, she got out, walked into the open grassland and started calling Samia's name. Within a minute we could see with the naked eye a great grey hulk trotting towards her.

Then an incredible reunion took place. As Anna and Samia met one another Anna put out her hand and placed it on Samia's horn. Samia put her head down to sniff the paper sack and, as the lifted it up, got her horn caught under Anna's skirt, raising it high. Anna tipped the horse-nuts on to the ground which Samia crunched while Anna rubbed her ears. We stayed in the Land Rover (Anna wasn't taking any chances with her guests) leaning out of the window to get as close a look as possible at this unique animal – Africa's rhino ambassador extraordinaire, much photographed as well as having been blessed by the Pope.

When Anna came back to the Land Rover, Samia followed, trying to get her head into the passenger window where I was sitting but luckily for me her great horn prevented her from doing so. However, I was able to get a wonderful picture of the side of her face with her great big eye in the middle. It was at this close range that we were able to see for ourselves her prominent prehensile upper lip. The black rhino is a browser, hence this lip, while the white is a grazer, having no such lip but a very wide mouth. The Afrikaans word for 'wide' is 'wyd' and, mispronounced, it became known as 'white'. The other became known as 'black' but both species are, in fact, plain grey.

Anna was then in her mid-sixties and had been living in Africa for the past 40 years. As a young bride, she and her first husband (also Swiss) went to live in Ghana where they set up their own engineering business. Anna became an Honorary Warden for the Game Department and was appalled to see how rapidly certain species of wildlife were disappearing. Her marriage broke up and she married her husband's boss, another Swiss. Twenty years later, when Karl retired, they went to live in Kenya.

In 1982 they took a holiday up at Lewa Downs, a 45,000 acre ranch in the foothills of Mount Kenya, owned by the Craig family. The ranch was not only home to several thousand head of cattle, but to vast herds of game grazing alongside them from elephant and giraffe to zebra and antelope. Some ten years earlier there had been no rhino here, too, but with the price of US $120,000 on the end of a rhino's nose, should it reach the Taiwanese marketplace for traditional Chinese medicine, it isn't surprising that most of them have been killed, shot with AK47s by marauding Somali poachers from over the border.

Anna told the Craigs of her intention to set up a rhino sanctuary to try to save this creature that had been around for some 65 million years, but in less than 25 years had been driven to the edge of extinction. The black rhino population had been reduced from 60,000 to just 2,500 in that time. The Craigs were keen to see the rhino reintroduced into their area and offered to lend Anna 5,000 acres. She sank her capital into building a simple house (we stayed in a nearby thatched 'rondavel'), stables, a manager's house and office, and put up electric fencing around the allotted area.

A year later she and Karl moved in but, of course, they had no rhinos. With the co-operation of the Kenya Wildlife Service's Capture Unit, they relocated rhinos at risk in neighbouring areas but first they had to be caught. No easy task. They were tranquillised with darts from a helicopter, dragged to a vehicle by sledge, given an antidote, transported back to the sanctuary and kept in holding pens until they had recovered the whole beastly business.

Anna had 36 rhinos – 20 black and 16 white – and the original sanctuary had been extended to include a forest reserve donated by the Government. All this had recently been amalgamated with the Craig's ranch under the umbrella banner of Lewa Wildlife Conservancy, employing a staff of 160. There are now 60,000 acres under electric fencing, monitored 24 hours a day by guards with walkie-talkies.

Ten years earlier Anna happened to see one of the black rhino cows actually giving birth. The mother then walked off, without so much as a backward glance. 'Probably because she had no milk due to a devastating drought we were having at the time' Anna says. Luckily for that new-born babe Anna was witness to its plight. She kept watch for two days and nights to protect it from lion and hyena and also to make sure that its mother didn't have second thoughts. She didn't and so Anna took the baby home. However, its body temperature was so low that to keep it warm, not only did she take it into her house but into her bed. It was a female calf and Anna named her Samia. She fed her on warm cow's milk from a 5-gallon plastic can with an improvised nozzle but it gave her violent diarrhea – in Anna's bed.

Never having been suckled by her mother, Samia was deficient in colostrum. Otherwise known as 'green milk', it is the very first milk secreted by a mammal after having given birth, supplying babies with antibodies to fight off infection as well as aiding digestion. In desperation Anna rang Daphne Sheldrick who has been rearing orphaned wildlife in Nairobi for over 30 years – my little Emily being

My brother Martin on
Prince, Frank, and me
on King, Dipford
Farm, Devon, 1940

Dorothy Brooke in the early 1930s with some of the original War Horses

Our wedding at Hampstead Parish
Church, April 1956

Angela with Harry the
Basset Hound on
Hampstead Heath, 1966

98

Martin with Cricket
in Australia

Anna Merz with Samia at Lewa Wildlife Conservancy, Kenya, 1995

99

Harry in the snow on Hampstead
Heath. winter 2000

Angela with chimp at
Chimfunshi, Zambia, 2000

100

Angela with baby llama in Peru, 2003

The Brooke vets at work in Cairo, October 2004

Anne Finch, Founder of Greyhounds in Need, with four rescued
Greyhounds (picture: Sally Anne Thompson)

Bear Hell. Martin and Angela standing by the rusty cages in which
the rescued bears were incarcerated

Bear Heaven. Two bears in their swimming-pool at Jill Robinson's
Moon Bear Sanctuary in Chengdu, China, April 2006

Celebrating our 50th wedding anniversary in a Moon Bear den

103

Virginia McKenna, Martin and Angela sitting on Elsa's grave,
Kenya 2009

Percy on Hampstead Heath, 2007

Juanita Carberry beside Miss Kenya

Capuchin monkey Joey at the Monkey Sanctuary in Cornwall

Angela and Martin standing by the cage in which Joey lived for
nine years in Hampstead, November 2008

Angela feeding a baby elephant at Daphne Sheldrick's Wildlife
Orphanage, Nr. Nairobi, Kenya. November 2009

106

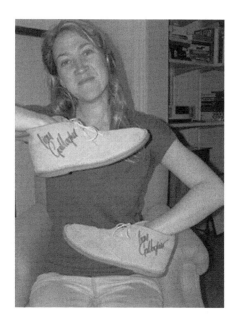

Amy Hanson with Liam Gallagher's shoes which I got for her

Peter Egan presenting us with Animals Asia Independent Volunteer(s)
Award, September 2013

Jill presenting Ricky Gervais with a picture of Moon Bear Derek, named after his current series 'Derek'

Fundraising lunch for International Animals Rescue's Orangutan Project in Borneo – Alan Knight of IAR; Amy Hanson of Small Steps Project; Ira Moss of All Dogs Matter; actor Peter Egan and my husband, Martin Humphery of Greyhounds in Need. summer 2013

Komodo Dragons, Komodo Island, Indonesia, February 2010

Angela and Great British Bake Off presenter, Sue Perkins,
promoting the very first national animal Wetnose Day

Our group of dog-owners up at Kenwood, April 2011

Wild Dog in Tanzania 2006

110

Iconic picture taken by Derek Cattani of Ace Bourke and John Rendall
with Christian the lion cub, Kings Road, Chelsea 1960

Stroking seal pup on the ice-floes, Magdalen Islands, Canada 1991

Feast of St. Francis, Blessing of the Beasts at The Cathedral of
St. John-the-Divine, New York City 1999

Holding up copies of Farmageddon at final tea-party for
Compassion in World farming, August 2014

Dame Judi Dench, our new Patron, taken at a chance meeting at
The Royal Geographical Society in September 2014

Our rescued 'galgo', Percy, with local celebrity Ricky Gervais
who is wearing a false nose to promote the very first national
Animal Wetnose Day August 2014

just one of the lucky ones. Daphne recommended a special formula for dairy sensitive children of vegetable oils and coconut milk. Samia ballooned from a mere 70lbs. to 200lbs. in just four months. Too big for Anna's bed, she was transferred to the stable. 'Everyone laughed' recalls Anna 'wrapped in a blanket she looked just like an armadillo'.

While showing us around, Anna opened the top half of the very stable once inhabited by Samia. That day it was home to a very different species, the guinea-pig. I counted fifty-seven. Seeing my surprise Anna laughed 'I eat them. They're my protein!' 'Crikey!' I gasped 'please don't give us guinea-pig for dinner, I used to have twenty-seven myself and they were my pets!'

When Samia was six months old Anna got a message from the President to take Samia down to the Masai Mara National Park so that the Pope, who was visiting Kenya at the time, would be photographed blessing her. Samia was duly crated up and flown south in a light-aircraft, barely able to get off the ground because of her weight. When she arrived back at the sanctuary she was a far from a healthy cow and it took Anna weeks of nursing to get her well again. All that trauma just to become a Holy Cow!

The following year Juanita and I went to one of the Monday evening lectures at The Royal Geographical Society which was of particular interest to Juanita since the lecturer was none other than Tony Fitzjohn, who Juanita knew well. Fitz was the young English renegade who had become George Adamson's assistant rehabilitating lions such as the famous two - Elsa and Christian. At the Q&A afterwards, I asked him how Anna Merz, Samia, and Samson, her calf, were faring.

I wasn't prepared for what he was about to tell me. 'They're both dead' he told us. 'One moonlit night both Samia and Samson fell over a cliff and when Anna discovered them in the morning, Samia was already dead but Samson was still alive – but with a broken back'. As if this news wasn't bad enough Fitz then added, ' Anna called Ian Craig who had no other option but to shoot the calf.' Anna was so devastated that she left Lewa and went to live in Melkrivier in South Africa's Northern Province where she founded a rhino museum. She died aged 81 on 4 April, 2013 just three and half months before Juanita.

I am so pleased that Anna died before learning that in South Africa alone a record 1,004 rhinos were poached for their horns in 2013 – an increase of over 59 per cent from 2012 - out of a total wild population of 20,000 - most of the world's population. Is it any wonder that this massacre is taking place when horn is now worth £40,000 a kilo in Asia.

Just before my close encounter with the rhino in Africa I was invited on a press trip to see the seal cubs on Canada's Magdalene Islands by IFAW (International Fund for Animal Welfare) headed by Brian Davies. The thought of these fluffy, cuddly creatures being clubbed to death over the next few weeks was unbearable. And for what – sealskin hats, gloves, coats and boots – which we can all perfectly well live without.

It was heads down and hands on for a tactile experience for both of us but one which scientists have proved has no lasting effect on the seals although the experience would stay with the humans for a lifetime. Seal watch might just as well be called seal kiss or seal cuddle.

Here we were, fifteen grown men and women wearing bright red onesies to keep us warm and to keep us visible should we fall into a snow-drift. In sub-zero temperatures, we were lying flat on our bellies on ice which was up to 3ft. thick in places, way out in the middle of the vast Gulf of St. Lawrence in Eastern Canada, kissing and cuddling baby seals.

A short helicopter flight out to the ice floes, on which huge herds of harp seals have floated south from the Arctic, brought us to a gigantic nursery. Here, each March, thousands of baby seals are born.

We marched across the ice, strung out single file in our red Father Christmas survival suits and white rubber boots, passing mother harp seals suckling their young. They raised their heads and barked at us not to come closer. Seconds later we came upon a lone 'whitecoat', the name by which seal pups are known for the first twelve days of their lives, then turning from milky white to dullish grey, wedged in a snowdrift.

Its mother had probably gone down a blowhole for a swim. Totally unafraid, its big black eyes stared up at us while huge tears rolled down its cheeks. In aaagh! ratings of 1-10, this was definitely a ten.

As we came in to land on the Magdalen Islands, a tiny archipelago in the middle of Canada's vast Gulf of St. Lawrence, no wonder the pilot of our helicopter looked amazed. 'Could you point out the nearest shopping-mall?' asked an American fellow seal watcher.

These dozen little islands are, undoubtedly, Quebec's (if not Canada's) best kept secret. Scenic and unspoilt, warmed by the waters of the Gulf Stream, they hardly have a shop, let alone a shopping-mall.

Home to some 15,000 Madelinots, eight of the islands are inhabited (six French speaking and two English) with just six being joined to one another by beautiful, long thin strips of sand, over which 65 miles of roadway have been built. It's perfect countryside for cycling (a traffic jam is two trucks nose-to-tail). Summer visitors take to pedal-power but there are also guided mini-bus tours and boat trips around the islands and light aircraft flights over them.

The English speaking Madelinots are descendants of shipwrecked survivors, mostly Scottish, while the French speakers are normally Acadian descendants. From 1755 the Acadians were dispossessed by Scottish settlers from what later became Nova Scotia (then known as l'Acadie) and scattered in all directions, heading for French-speaking regions such as Louisiana and Quebec.

Although geographically part of the Maritime Provinces, politically the Magdalen Islands are an outpost of Quebec, which means that the local cuisine has a distinctly French flavour – and all the better for that.

The seafood is mouth-watering although I did draw the line at flipper-pie. But it isn't just the cuisine on the Maggies which is mouth-watering. The colours of the houses and the landscape are too.

Clapboard houses, painted in shades of raspberry, blueberry, blancmange, saffron and peppermint, dot the rolling countryside while the cliffs are the colour of chocolate, the hundred or so miles of beaches and sand-dunes, the hue of cappuccino coffee, the valleys several shades of green and the lagoons a brilliant blue.

The beautiful snow-white church at La Verniere on Ile du Cap-aux-Meules (otherwise known as Grindstone Island) where we stayed is one of the most important wooden structures still standing in North America today. Lines of brightly coloured washing blow in the breeze outside every clapboard home.

Hikers and horse-riders, photographers and painters, bird-watchers and wind-surfers, mollusc diggers and deep-sea divers throng here in the summer when the seawater and lagoon temperatures range from 17c to 20c.

But we, of course, were there in winter. Apart from the attraction of seal watch the Magdalens take on a magical glow. The snow starts to melt, then freezes, turning patches of water into myriad mirrors which sparkle in the sunshine.

I heard later from anti-fur campaigning group 'Respect for Animals' that over recent years Madeleine Islanders' sealers have dumped some 6,000 skins in the sea due to lack of demand as well as the fact that seal skins can no longer be processed on the islands, the last processing company there closing its doors following a fire. The impact of the EU ban on seal imports has also reduced their markets. So perhaps things are changing and there is hope that this annual carnage of seal pups will cease.

Towards the end of the 1990s I went on a press trip, a 'Treasures of Central India' tour with a company specialising in 'adventure travel'. Falling out of Bombay airport and into the arms of our tour leader, we were shell-shocked.

In the streets, on traffic islands and roundabouts, in the shops and on the beaches – Holy Cow – they are everywhere! Known as 'brake inspectors', woe betide any scooter, rickshaw, car or truck that hits one of these sacred creatures. Sacred cows they may be, but their plight seems to be to wander will-nilly, subsisting on a diet of newspaper and plastic bags.

Owing to the late arrival of our flight, we had just a few hours to take a quick look at this gigantic city before being whisked off to one of India's great Gothic buildings, the Victoria Terminus, for yet another hard day's night – a ten-hour rail journey to Aurangabad to see the world-famous cave temples of Ajanta and Ellora. The window had a hole through which cold air streamed into our compartment. My husband, lying frozen on the top bunk, moaned that this was meant to be a holiday.

After these two magnificent caves it was time for another overnight train journey but, forewarned is forearmed. We bought blankets at £2 apiece, but worth their weight in gold. We arrived in Hyderabad at dawn and, having fought to get on the train, we fought to get off again, too. In fact, the train started pulling out of the station with three of our party still on board. They actually had to jump off with all their luggage.

It was here in Hyderabad's Golconda mines that the Koh-i-Noor diamond was found. Not surprisingly, there were no diamonds for us but a visit to the Golconda Fort, towering 120 metres above its 16th century battlements, followed by a trip to the Night Market. This vast shopping arena is an insomniac's dream, where you can find anything from saris to sugarcane, cricket bats to bicycles.

Our next stop was the medieval walled city of Bijapur, dominated by the Gol Gumbaz, a vast 17th-century mausoleum with a

38-metre diameter dome, the second largest after St. Peter's in Rome. We watched the sunrise from here, listening to the echoes in its whispering gallery, then back to the hotel for a shower, and breakfast in the garden. The shower was Indian-style – that is to say, a boy brings big buckets of hot water to your room, with a small plastic jug clipped on to the side of the bucket. It is this jug that turns the bucket of hot water into a shower. Breakfast is also Indian-style. We wait for ages, eventually tapping our watches. The waiter smiles. 'It is coming, it is coming', he cries, 'but slowly'.

Our final architectural wonder and, to my mind, the highlight of the tour, was the magnificent site of Hampi, surrounded by 20 miles of dry-stone walling. Once the flourishing capital of the Vihayanagar kings, who ruled one of the largest Hindu empires in Indian history, it was destroyed in battle in 1565. Set amid a desolate boulder-strewn landscape, these ancient ruins include the Queen's Bath (the size of a swimming pool) and the vast vaulted Elephant Stables, that once housed eleven of these great beasts.

From Badami a 12-hour bus-ride took us over the Western Ghats down into the tiny, lush, green and prosperous state of Goa. A Portuguese colony between 1510 and 1961, the city of Old Goa, the former capital, is said to have rivalled Lisbon in its splendour. After two weeks of exploring Hindu temples and Muslim Mosques, we now found ourselves in Catholic cathedrals, such as the Basilica of Bom Jesus, wherein lie the remains of St. Francis of Xavier, the 15th century Jesuit missionary who gave the region its Christianity.

I was thinking more of St. Francis of Assisi, patron saint of animals, on our guided tour rather than the Jesuit missionary and his relics. The holy cows on the beach looked a pitiful sight but it was the street dogs that really upset me. Worse was to come. A bald puppy caught my eye. There was not a single hair on its body and covered with mange, it lay under the shade of a scrubby hedge. I pleaded with our guide to find a vet to put it down, which I said I'd pay for. I was duly put in touch with one and handed over a mere £20 for this poor mite's destruction.

Then one of our group, who had been witness to my transaction with the vet, gave me a flyer handed to her by two English girls working in Goa for a charity called International Animal Rescue (IAR). Had I known about them a few hours earlier, I would have alerted them to the plight of the puppy which could probably have been saved.

IAR was founded in 1988, the very same year as was BDMLR whose founder director, Alan Knight, was also instrumental in founding IAR. When I came back to England I gave him a ring and a decade later we renewed contact and I have been an avid supporter of IAR ever since.

The charity started work in Goa in a small way working in a rented bungalow and sterilising street dogs on the kitchen table. IAR Goa now has its own rescue centre with six resident vets, and well over 15,000 dogs and 8,000 cats have now been inoculated against rabies.

However, their main claim to fame has been the rescue of all the dancing bears in India. They rescued the last dancing bear in December 2009 after a seven-year campaign to stop the terrible suffering of these magnificent creatures. This victory could never have been accomplished without the help of the Indian charity Wildlife SOS. Together with Free the Bears in Australia and One Voice of France, they all worked together to save the Sloth bears of India.

Sloth bears are so called because their long curved claws resemble those of a sloth. To turn them into 'dancing bears' young bears are captured in the wild, separated from their mothers, and taught by a trainer to become dancing bears in condition of unimaginable cruelty. The young animals are forced onto sheets of glowing hot metal and, in order to escape the pain, the bears alternate lifting up one paw and then another while music is played. The process is repeated again and again until the animals automatically begin to raise their paws - to 'dance' - in fear of the pain, even when there are no metal sheets.

As the bears get older the trainers keep them under control by inflicting pain. They do this by putting rings through the bears' highly sensitive noses and jaws. No anaesthetic is used for this painful process. Chains are attached to the rings so that the trainers can control the animals, which weigh up to 350 kilograms, with only a slight tug on the chains.

The bear's claws are trimmed several times a year and their teeth broken or removed so they can't injure their trainer. The bears also suffer from an inadequate diet that usually consists of white bread, sugar and alcohol. All these cause serious physical health problems for the bears. Many also display stereotypic behaviours such as swaying and pacing and self-mutilation as they cannot follow natural behavioural patterns and instincts.

Here, Alan Knight describes how he and his charity managed to put a stop to the dancing bear trade which had been going on since the days of the Mogul empire in the 18th century.

Alan said, 'The Kalandar gypsies originally danced their bears in the courts, and this gradually expanded to a general entertainment spectacle and tourist attraction. We had to have three things on our side to stop the trade. The law had to be on our side and luckily here we had the Wildlife Act of 1972 which made dancing bears illegal. We also had to have the Government on our side

'Then we needed sanctuaries to house the animals, and funding to keep them there for the rest of their lives. IAR and Free the Bears provided three sanctuaries with 250 acres to house the bears.

Finally we needed the Kalandar community to accept our retraining package which included retraining them in a different profession that did not include cruelty to animals. It took a long time to get their trust, bur the last dancing bear walked into our sanctuary in 2009. It took us seven years to finish a trade that had been going on for 300 years.'

Alan Knight (now OBE) also set up the charity 'Yayasan IAR Indonesia' and they have the largest Slow Loris rescue centre in the world with over 100 lorises waiting for release into the wild. They also have a macaque rescue and rehab centre in Java and an orangutan rescue and rehab. and release centre in Kalimantan with over 80 orangutans currently in residence.

Alan's latest plan is to secure large areas of rainforest from the devastating palm oil industry and provide security patrols to protect the forest so that it can provide a long tern home for the orangutan and all of the other animals and plants that call the rainforest home.

Yet another charity that I support is WDCS – the Whale and Dolphin Conservation Society, so I was delighted to go on a whale-watching trip to Quebec at the end of the 1990s.

We saw what looked like little puffs of smoke rising from the surface of the estuary but, as we got nearer, we could see they were great jets of water shooting skywards – spray from the blowholes of the whales we'd come to watch in Quebec. It was a cold grey morning out in the St. Lawrence River and we were clinging for dear life to the sides of our 12-seater Zodiac inflatable – a bucking bronco rising up and crashing down in the waves. Suddenly, finbacks and minkes appeared all around us, so close that we could almost reach out and touch them. There are humpbacks and great blues here, too, as well as belugas, the white, hard-boiled egg look-alikes.

It seemed as though a fleet of submarines were closing in on us, at any moment their periscopes rising up to inspect us closer. But these gentle giants of the deep are people-friendly, surprisingly so since in many parts of the world they have been hunted almost to extinction. 'They know exactly where we are, and certainly won't overturn us', shouted our skipper above the roar of the engine. That was reassuring news since blue whales are the largest animals in existence.

At 8am down at the dockside in Tadoussac we pulled on thermal hats and gloves, yellow waterproofs and gumboots. This pretty little port and whale-watching capital of Quebec stands where the St. Lawrence and Saguenay rivers meet, a fast-food outlet for whales because of the vast amounts of krill and caplin living in these plankton-rich waters. It was also one of the first French settlements in North America, the first fur-trading post in Canada and home to the country's oldest wooden church, constructed in 1747 under the direction of Fr. Coquan, a Jesuit missionary. Tadoussac is also home to the Marine Mammals Interpretation Centre where we learned about these amazing creatures from skeletons, slide shows, photographs and film.

From whale-watching in the rough waters of the St. Lawrence seaway, our next taste of wildlife was over on the Gaspe peninsula, a tongue of land lying to the east of Quebec City which juts out into the Atlantic between the lower reaches of the St. Lawrence and the Baie des Chaleurs. Shaped like the head of a giant salmon (king here with twenty six salmon rivers), this is an undiscovered corner of Quebec full of surprises – 300 miles in length, with mountains in the middle, and 600 miles of coastline dotted with pretty little fishing villages with brightly coloured light-houses.

On our way back to Montreal we stopped for the night in Metis-su-Mer, on the northern shore of the Gaspe, not only to see the famous gardens there but to dine at Au Coin de la Baie, an award-winning restaurant. 'Chevaline' was on the menu that night, the waitress asking if we would 'ave ze 'orse'. 'Non, merci!' was our reply!

Although French by name and cuisine, this village was, in fact, founded by Scots, with street names such as McNider and McLaren being dead giveaways. In 1802 Matthew McNider bought the seigneurie of Metis and, being a bachelor, left it to his nephew John. In 1818 John proceeded to establish a colony bring settlers from Scotland at his own expense.

Kipper ties and cod-pieces aren't news but sole and salmon slippers, turbot belts and bomber jackets, haddock hats and handbags most certainly are. Should you be looking for strange souvenirs of the Gaspe, the town of Bonaventure will oblige, being the only place in the whole of Quebec where you can buy garments and goodies made from fish leather.

At the tip of the peninsula we came upon the town of Gaspe where Jacques Cartier first took possession of New France in 1534, a monument and cross marking this historic spot. Nearby Forillon National Park is a wild place of forests and prairies, dunes and marshes, zigzag cliffs and spectacular headlands. For those who can be seasick just looking at a sailor, help is at hand; you can see giant humpbacks breaching as you hike along the cliff edge.

Further south lies the tiny town of Perce, famous for its spectacular rock rising out of the sea, a six million-tonne mammoth with a hole in the middle, carved by the wind and water over 350 million years. Echoing off the rock is the incessant shrieking of thousands of gulls and gannets on Ile Bonaventure, classified in 1985 as a conservation park and the largest bird sanctuary in North America with some 60,000 northern gannets nesting here every year.

We took a boat trip over to the island to get a closer look at these birds which get such a bad press for their voracious appetites. The noise and the smell of this vast colony is quite over powering. The ground was wall-to-wall gannets while, up above, the sky was grey with them, flying off to fish and then returning to feed their hungry young. Born naked, gannet chicks grow white down and then grey feathers before turning into snow-white adults, if they're lucky: 4% die on these cliffs and 80% never make their first birthday. When the adults leave around the end of September for the warmer waters of the Gulf of Mexico, those chicks under three months old which aren't up to the journey are left behind to starve to death. Life at the top (of a cliff) is tough!

The house attached to ours in Hampstead has always been problematic. It is split into four flats with four Flying Freeholds, therefore no interlocking covenants. Nobody is responsible for the Common Parts and therefore the house looks somewhat neglected.

One tenant, an alcoholic, had a Persian cat to which he was feeding bird-seed rather than Whiskas or whatever. I managed to get his father to rehome the poor animal before it grew wings and took flight but no sooner than had that problem been solved than I saw through his ground-floor window, two tiny kittens asleep on a chair.

Not long afterwards his brother-in-law rang to say he'd been taken to hospital. When I asked what had happened to his two kittens, he said there weren't any kittens there. Having a key I went to check it out for myself. No kittens in the kitchen, no kittens in the living-room, no kittens in the bedroom and no kittens in the bathroom. Relieved, I was about to leave but when opening the front-door I heard faint mewing from under the floor-boards. They had somehow got underneath the cupboard in the hallway and I couldn't coax them out.

I rang a friend who worked for Cats' Protection and she came round with a tin of kipper pate. Frightened by the loud music the previous evening, they had gone behind the cooker, taking refuge in a pipe. Starving by then, the kipper pate did the trick. However, their saviour was unable to take them home as her house was already full of rescued cats and asked me to look after them for the weekend. That weekend became sixteen years.

One was a black and white queen, hence the name Queenie, and the other a black half-Siamese. As I had just taken a photographic course we called him Kodak. Queenie was the more adventurous of the two, running up the curtains with alarming speed or using the square handles on the drawers in the kitchen as a ladder to get up on to the worktop, where I fed them so that the dog didn't steal their dinner.

One day Kodak leapt up on to the worktop but misjudged it and landed on the hot-plate which was still hot. He let out a piercing yowl, having burned the pads on his paws. He never did that again. Kodak was the first to go being put down at twelve, the vet asking if he could perform an autopsy since he wasn't able to diagnose his illness. He was clearly in pain, hiding in strange places. The autopsy revealed an unusual form of cancer.

Queenie then became top dog or rather, top cat, replacing Kodak who had been the boss. She lived till sixteen when, like many cats her kidneys went into meltdown, and so severe was her weight loss that prior to putting her down the vet suggested some appetite stimulants. Giving a cat oral medication is no easy job. Having been caught and then wrapped in a towel to prevent her from escaping or scratching us, Queenie then required someone to hold her tight while another, wearing heavy-duty industrial gloves, popped the pill into her mouth while massaging her throat to make the medicine go down. Once released she'd then spit it out!

However, she became so terrified that she'd hide under the sofa when she saw the towel being brought out. We decided that there was no point in extending her life if giving her the medication was so traumatising, so we stopped and it wasn't long before she went to join the boss.

*   *   *

In 1999, we went Down Under to take a look at New South Wales and while there in Sydney, I read about a koala hospital up the coast in Port Macquarie. We made an appointment, there to be greeted by the chief honcho, none other than a childhood friend of Martin's from Sanderstead, Surrey, who showed us around the hospital.

Cricket was an orphan. Cute and cuddly, he had large brown eyes, a big black shiny nose and huge fluffy ears. He was found six months earlier with his ailing mother in Port Macquarie, both being brought to the hospital of the Koala Preservation Society, in the grounds of the Macquarie Nature Reserve, where John and Judy Dielman, Cricket's adoptive parents, work.

'The mother died', Judy told me, 'but Cricket survived because he'd already left the pouch as she had no milk'. The suspicion was that as koalas eat dirt around ants' nests the mother might have been poisoned. People put down poison for ants in Australia. The Dielmans fell in love with the koala the day they first caught sight of him, which was the day Australia won the Ashes. So they called him Cricket.

Cricket was lucky. For most koalas, being cute and cuddly is no guarantee of survival, though it has been the first Australian animal to be protected by law. Yet their habitat is being bulldozed for development, they get squashed on the roads, are drowned in swimming-pools, savaged by dogs, sucked dry by ticks and burned alive in bush fires.

On top of it all, koalas are prone to a viral infection which causes conjunctivitis, pneumonia and sterility, and bowel and bladder disorders resulting in such descriptive conditions as 'dirty tail' and 'wet bottom', which can kill.

Before taking a personal interest in the koala, John and Judy Dielman had raised dozens of orphaned kangaroos in addition to fostering over 200 children. Then Judy started working with the Koala Preservation Society, founded in 1973. She began nursing koalas, which needed 24-hour intensive care and couldn't be left overnight at the hospital.

'I began taking them into my own home' she said. 'I became so involved that two-and-a-half years ago I came to work in the hospital permanently.Her husband, John, was in charge of food supplies. Cricket traveled around in the car with him, clinging to his head. 'Yes', he said, 'people do double-takes when they glimpse me at traffic lights or crossings. He clings to the back of my head because that's where baby koalas hang on to their mothers when they leave the pouch at six months old'.

'At night Cricket even sleeps with us, still clinging to my head', laughed John 'but sits up when I turn over', adding proudly 'but he's never once wet the bed'.

Although often referred to as a 'koala bear', the koala is a marsupial, not related to the bear at all. It may be distantly related to the wombat, which resembles a large brindle guinea-pig.

The koala is a rather poorly designed creature. You could kill it with a cuddle, so exposed are its lungs and heart on account of an open rib-cage. Its diet is highly specialised, eating only a certain species of leaf, almost exclusively the eucalyptus. The leaves of the gum tree, however, are so low in nutritional value that the koala must move around at a sloth-like pace to conserve energy. For around eighteen out of every twenty-four hours, it is fast asleep.

When born, in an embryonic state after a mere 38-35 days gestation, the cub is the size of a peanut. Though bind and lacking fur, it has arms strong enough to enable it to crawl up to its mother's pouch which, unlike that of the kangaroo has a vertical opening. It then attaches itself to one of two teats available, to emerge after six or seven months to face the world.

Efforts were being made to save the koala. On the roads round Port Macquarie for instance, we saw bright yellow signs tacked on to telegraph poles warning KOALAS ON ROADS IN TOWN AREA. Each had a silhouette of a koala clinging to a wooden telegraph pole. There was no lack of volunteers in this small town (founded in 1821 and a penal settlement until 1830) to nurse and feed koala patients on special formula diets. It's great to see these little animals swaddled in thick towels so that their long sharp claws do not scratch the hand that feeds them. At the sight of the eyedropper they opened their mouths like good children.

Judy Stace, one of the volunteer nurses at the hospital was positively beaming the afternoon we were there. She was holding one, O'Sullivan (recovering from a broken jaw) in her arms and said, 'I haven't nursed him for two weeks and now, on giving him his formula, he rubbed his nose up and down my cheek. That makes working here well worthwhile'.

When recovered, O'Sullivan along with the other koalas will be released back into the wild. Cricket will go too when he's about 18 months old' said John rather sadly. He'll certainly miss his little head-warmer.

Later we met Dr. Steve Brown, Research Director of the Bond University-based Centre for Wildlife Research on Australia's Gold Coast, said if you can't save the cute and cuddly creatures, what chance have the ugly ones got?'

On a subsequent trip Down Under, this time on the opposite side of the continent, we went to swim with the dolphins at Shark Bay in Western Australia. There aren't many places in the world where in just one day you can pat a dingo, cuddle a kangaroo, have your toes tickled by wild dolphins and walk on a blindingly white, crunchy beach made up entirely of billions of tiny bi-valve shells. All these tactile experiences we enjoyed up on the Peron Peninsula, some 500 miles north of Perth.

Most tourists headed for Shark Bay, as we did, where at Monkey Mia there are neither sharks nor monkeys, but a resident pod of eight bottle-nose dolphins. Under the supervision of two rangers you can feed, stroke and swim with these intelligent and friendly creatures.

Standing knee-deep in the clear waters of this unspoilt bay waiting for the dolphins to appear, Tom Pepper, the Aboriginal ranger, told me about Shell Beach and newly opened Nanga Wildlife Park, run by Australia's then Mother Earth, Dott Terry.

But first things first. The dolphins. When they arrived there was utter hush as they swam up close and personal. I lowered my hand into the warm water and touched one. Its skin felt like a shelled hard-boiled egg. They stayed with us for at least fifteen minutes while we fed and stroked them and clicked away on our cameras.

Later down at Nanga Wildlife Park we met Dott Terry, wearing a battered old Akubra on her head and a pair of rubber thongs on her feet, who greeted us like old friends. Currently in her care were 36 mammals, from kangaroos, wallabies and possums to a pair of dingoes plus four Tawny Frogmouths (related to the kookaburra) and a Nankeen kestrel. All were abandoned, injured or orphaned and without Dott's constant tender loving care, none would have survived.

'It's been a dream all these years,' Dott confessed as she introduced me to some of her 26 kangaroos 'to be able to run a wildlife park of my own, keeping animals that are unsuitable for releasing back into the their natural environment'.

Now that dream has come true, she has taken a course in wildlife veterinary surgery, because what few vets there are in this sparsely populated state know nothing about wildlife. Locals now come to her with their domestic animals. However, her speciality is the kangaroo which, despite being Australia's national emblem, often suffers a harsh fate. It is run down on the roads and shot by farmers.

Twins Bill and Ben were a typical example. 'Their mother was shot while they were still in the pouch and, since they were so small, I had to rear them in incubators'. Dott was an expert at this practice.

Because she is known never to turn away any creature, some non-indigenous species have crept in, such as ducks and a blind swan (one of the ducks acts as its seeing eye) donkeys, goats and a fox – foxes being brought into Australia by early British settlers to be hunted. Recently a pair of camels and two starving horses were brought to her - the horses costing more to feed than all the others put together. Dott received no government funding, her overheads coming out of the capital from the sale of her family house.

Around Christmas 1992 they sold up at Mandurah, bought a caravan and headed north to the Peron Peninsula where they leased 10 acres from a sheep station. 'Transporting 80 animals in trailers from Mandurah to Nanga was quite an adventure' laughed Dott. Since they opened in 1993, over 2,000 people, including local schoolchildren, have visited Nanga. Education is high on their agenda.

My first reaction was that these creatures must be her surrogate children, but not so. She and her husband Jim (from Sheffield) have had seven children of their own and fostered many others. One of four children Dott, was born Dorothy Matthews in 1944 in Western Australia and grew up in Glen Forest in the hills above Perth. 'Nature was always on my doorstep' she says. 'My life revolved around animals and my parents taught me to take responsibility for something other than myself'.

That childhood training has stood her in good stead. Twenty years ago, when her youngest children were still babies, she began caring for the injured and orphaned wildlife which Jim brought home from around the mining area where he worked. 'Although he doesn't have a hands-on approach, he's been very caring, creative, patient and supportive over the years.' She told me proudly. Their house in Mandurah often had bassinettes full of fluffy marsupials which would drink from a baby's bottle and wear disposable nappies. When the Terry family went visiting, the animals went too.

Pointing to an empty cage, Dott said its occupant had flown the nest only the previous day. A year ago a mountain duck had been brought in to her as a tiny duckling, its family having been run over. 'Yesterday, it flapped its wings, took off and flew south. Jim and I both cried', she said. 'We were both glad and sad because it had once saved my life – one day I felt a tiny bird pecking at my feet and when I looked down there was a deadly brown snake right in front of me'.

While on an Aussie high, having been east and then west, it was time to take a walk on the wild side up north – where it really is wild.

It was love at first sight for my husband. Tall and slim Gabrielle, the ranger, did look divine in her Kakadu National Park uniform of bottle green shirt and trousers, boots, bush hat and long silver earrings. So I quite understood. For me it was love at first sight, too.

From a striped rucksack, tossed nonchalantly over Gabrielle's shoulder, a small and inquisitive furry face popped out.

'This is Skin,' she said, introducing a baby wallaby to our group, which she was about to take on a walk up to Waterfall Creek, adding, 'she's called Skin because when I found her in her dead mother's pouch by the roadside, she was so young that she had no fur.'

We climbed to the top of the escarpment, where there was a spectacular panoramic view for miles and miles around and two gin-clear natural plunge-pools, one with a waterfall pouring into it, the other spilling over the edge of the escarpment, forming another waterfall. Designer pools in luxury resorts seldom look this good. No wonder this magical place was chosen for location shots for the film 'Crocodile Dundee'. Gabrielle told us that before it was made in the early Eighties, no more than 10,000 tourists a year came to the park. Now the figure (1996) is closer to 230,000.

One of Australia's natural marvels, Kakadu is wedged between the East and West Alligator Rivers which flow into the Van Diemen Gulf at the Top End of Australia's Northern Territory. (The rivers were misnamed by an early British explorer after seeing the river's prolific crocodile population). A third of the size of Tasmania, covering almost 7,720 square miles, it is designated a World Heritage site.

The name Kakadu comes from Gagadju, one of the local Aboriginal languages – part of Kakadu is Aboriginal land, leased to the government for use as a national park.

There are several types of kangaroo and wallaby in the park and that evening a mob of wallabies hopped through our campsite, stopping to stare as we sat around the fire having dinner. For a moment they looked as though they were going to join us, but thought better of it.

There are twenty-five species of bat and the strange little sugar glider – a squirrel-like creature with a webbed flange joining fore-leg to hind-leg, enabling it to 'glide' through the air from branch to branch.

In 1979, when Kakadu became a national park, there were also 400,000 water buffalo here, introduced from Timor during the early settlements in the 1820s up on the Cobourg Peninsular to the north-east of Darwin. By 1845 the settlements were abandoned and about 50 buffalo set free. They soon made up the largest wild population in the world, causing widespread environmental damage. In the 1980s their numbers were reduced as part of a national brucellosis and tuberculosis eradication programme. There are now no more than one hundred in the entire park.

After a five o'clock wake-up call we caught the dawn river cruise around Yellow Waters billabong, a wetlands region that is home to many of the 250 species of bird found in Kakadu. There were ibis and owls, cormorants and kingfishers, pelicans and darters, herons and egrets, rainbow bee-eaters and red-tailed black cockatoos, sea eagles and wedge-tailed eagles, whistling kites and black kites, brolgas and bustards. It was like being in a gigantic aviary.

Yellow Waters is not only a paradise for birdwatchers, at dawn it is a paradise for photographers too. As the sun rose, we saw skeins of magpie geese, of which there are some four million here, and an egret came into land, silhouetted against the great orange ball of the sun. It was mid-May at the time and flocks of birds were just coming back into these flood-plains after 'the wet' – the monsoon rains that fall from the beginning of October to the end of April.

It was hard to believe that back in January the car parks were all under water. With so much water there are twenty-five species of frog, seventy-five sorts of fish (including the three-foot long silver barramundi which changes sex from male to female at round five years of age), and seventy-seven kinds of reptile, from water snakes to freshwater crocodiles, considered to be less dangerous;, and some 3,500 of the lethal saltwater variety in the park. They can stay down in the water for up to two hours and grow about one foot a year for the first five hears of their lives. 'Freshies' live up to a mere fifty years, while 'salties' can reach the ripe old age of eighty-five.

As our boat glided silently along, we passed meadows of water-lilies, men fishing from canoes, birds perched on the skeleton of a dead tree and, best of all, a gigantic 'salty' slithering out of the water on to a nearby bank. It then lay there, just a few feet away, vast mouth wide open in a perfect pose for a picture. It didn't bat an eyelid as shutters clicked and camcorders whirred.

This is real crocodile country – there is even a crocodile farm in Darwin with 8,000 of these creatures. You can watch them being fed, then buy a handbag or wallet made from their skin. We took a Jungle Cruise aboard the Adelaide River Queen, when 'The Original Famous Jumping Crocodiles' actually jumped out of the water, stood on their hind legs and begged for food – just like a dog!

There is a hotel within Kakadu built to look like a gigantic crocodile and a 'Hard Croc Café up on the Arnhem Highway; just over the border in Western Australia is Wyndham, known as the home of ' The Big Croc'. A sign there says 'Please Do Not Climb on The Crocodile'. At the entrance to the town a 60ft. long crocodile stands ten feet high, a replica of the 'salties' which frequent the Cambridge Gulf on which the port of Wyndham lies.

Wherever there is water in Australia's North West there are signs against swimming – 'Don't Risk Your Life'. No one knows this better than our driver/guide, Antoine Shultz, a wiry little Frenchman who had lived in the Outback for twenty years. A couple of years earlier, he was dropped off to spend a day swimming in a lake that he knew to be free of 'salties'. However, he had a close encounter with a so-called friendly 'freshy' there, which sank its teeth into his arm. Managing to free himself from its jaws, he was able to swim ashore and staunch the bleeding by making a tourniquet with his shirt, luckily being picked up later and rushed to hospital.

Eat your heart out Crocodile Dundee – Crocodile Shultz is the real deal, and has scars to prove it!

To complete the four corners of Australia, I needed to do the south and was thrilled to be invited on a press trip to Tasmania, Australia's very own Down Under. This green and pleasant land – with a Brighton and a Bridgewater, a Sheffield and a Swansea, as well as a taste for cream teas – is the last place on earth where you'd expect to come face to face with a devil, let alone a tiger. Tasmania is full of surprises.

Just twenty-five minutes from Hobart, the state capital, is the Bonorong Park Wildlife Centre. Way back in 1996 Robert Douglas was the owner of this wildlife sanctuary, who proudly introduced us to his family. I've seldom seen such paternal devotion, which isn't too surprising since he has hand-reared his marsupial orphans, from koalas and kangaroos to pademelons and potoroos. Sadly, there was no sign of the elusive Tasmanian tiger, a meat-eating marsupial with the head of a wolf, the striped body of a tiger, and sloping hyena-like hindquarters. The last one in captivity died in Beaumaris Zoo, Hobart, in 1936 and, although there have been reported sightings since then, it's now thought to be extinct.

Not so the strange, ugly little Tasmanian devil, a creature about the size of a small Jack Russell but with the jaws of a pit-bull terrier – only ten times stronger. When Douglas climbed into the devils' den with a bucket of freshly killed rabbits, a youngster grabbed a great chunk and ran off, returning seconds later for another chunk. It had devoured it with the speed of a hot knife going through butter – fur, bones, guts and all.

'If you don't like the weather, wait five minutes!' say the locals. Although, in general, the climate is similar to ours, in just one week I was snowed on while walking around Lake Dove in the Cradle Mountain-Lake St. Clair National Park, and scorched by the sun while hiking up to the lookout over Wine Glass Bay in Freycinet National Park. Umbrella and thermals, sunglasses and sunblock – I needed the lot.

Named Van Dieman's Land in 1642 by Abel Tasman, this apple-shaped (and apple growing) island, no larger than the Irish Republic, boasts barely half a million souls. It's green and mountainous, with ancient forest and alpine meadows. Like many islands, it's a time-warp with magnificent colonial homesteads and quaint villages. Richmond, twenty-four kilometres from Hobart, is Tasmania's most historic town, with more than fifty buildings dating from the 19th century. It also contains the nation's oldest road bridge, built by convicts in 1823 – in Tasmania, anything 'colonial convict-built' is advertised with pride.

In the south-east of the island is the Tasman Peninsula, where the prison town of Port Arthur stands. Australia's most infamous penal settlement is now Tasmania's premier tourist attraction.

Eaglehawk Neck, a one hundred metre wide strip of land, was the only escape route for inmates. It was guarded day and night by mastiffs while a rumour was put about that the sea was alive with sharks. From 1830 to 1877, this solitary outpost of human deprivation housed prisoners transported from Britain. Some were political prisoners, others had stolen a loaf of bread. Among them were children – some as young as nine.

To complement the history you see during the day, you can stay in up-market 'colonial heritage' B&Bs where four-poster beds and antique furniture blend with present-day comforts such as spa baths. The roads are empty and they drive on the left. You could easily lapse into believing you were back in dear Old Blighty if it wasn't for those dear little devils!

It was 1999. All New York was there, including famous photographer Richard Avedon, German and Japanese TV crews, foreign snappers and locals of all creeds and colours. Standing on Amsterdam Avenue on Manhattan's Upper West Side, the imposing Cathedral Church of St. John the Divine (third largest house of worship in the world) is the mother church of the Episcopal Diocese of New York and the Seat of its Bishop.

On the first Sunday of October it was packed to the rafters with some 4,000 people as well as 400 animals, congregating for this the 14th Blessing of the Beasts for the Feast of St. Francis Earth Mass, held here every year since 1985. St. Francis of Assisi is, of course, the patron saint of animals.

My New York photographer who'd told me about this annual event suggested my husband and I went along the previous day to ask the co-ordinator of media/volunteers/animals for a press pass. Having tracked her down in this vast cathedral, we explained we'd come all the way from England specially for this ceremony. Press passed assured, she then made us an offer we couldn't refuse. 'You are staying this morning to help, aren't you?'

Ushering us into a large room she showed us a huge pile of bright red ecclesiastical robes, pointing to a steamer bubbling away in the corner. Forty-eight robes in all – one for each of those in the procession bringing an animal to be blessed. We set to work – my husband never having ironed so much as a handkerchief, let alone a shirt, since his army days.

There were about half a dozen of us so-called 'volunteers': a Cherokee Indian woman mending holes, a Chinese girl from London, an Afro-Caribbean girl and a Jewish ex US Navy guy hemming the robes, which had to be cut down to fit kids. He said he'd made many a flag while in the Service and I assumed him to be a master tailor. In fact, although his Jewish jokes were terrific, his tailoring was a disaster. And, of course there we WASPS were on the steamer and ironing board. A broad church, you might say! The good news was that coffee, bagels and cream cheese, without which no New Yorker can survive for long, were freely available.

Next morning, as directed, we reported in at nine, two hours before the service began. There was already a long queue outside. I heaved a terrific sigh of relief as we were led in through a back door and up onto the photographers' stand. A skinny little guy with thick silver hair was flitting about. 'That's Richard Avedon!' someone whispered, as lenses were turned on him and shutters clicked.

It was a sunny autumn Sunday and Miss Understood, a nine-year-old boa constrictor from the Turtle Back Zoo in West Orange, New Jersey, was there for her umpteenth annual blessing. Huey, the camel stood silently chewing the cud. His carer, hair long and flowing, reminded me of a biblical character. Farfel, a disgruntled looking, 30-year old Tawny Frogmouth (an Australian bird) was not only the oldest creature there but the oldest of its species in captivity while Baby, an iguana, garlanded in fresh flowers, winked a hooded eye, posing like an old pro with her proud owner. A pretty 10-year-old girl held up the head of her 12-year-old python, Tiny, whose body was coiled, scarf-like, around her neck.

Crowds had been queuing since seven that morning for tickets – available free at the door at nine – for the two-hour service, scheduled to start at eleven. Pews were filling up with people while their pet poodles and boxers, Clumber, Springer and King Charles spaniels and mongrels lay curled at their feet while rabbits and tortoises, cats and kittens were being nursed in children's arms. Cages of budgerigars, canaries and parakeets were parked in the aisles, and I could see a particularly well-behaved macaw perched quietly on a girl's shoulder.

Below a sign marked 'BIG DOGS', a Rottweiler menacingly eyed up a standard poodle, while an Old English sheepdog snored its head off. But all of a sudden these three seemed not-so-big as a gigantic canine (yellow Labrador, Deerhound/German Shepherd cross) called Whoppa, collapsed with a sigh on to the floor, spreading himself across not only at his master's feet but several other people's, too.

Then it was lift-off as the festival choir broke into song. The music, composed for the occasion, resembled the sound of whales calling and lions roaring. Girls in white leotards wafted about on the stage in front of the altar; then came African dancers on stilts and priests swinging incense burners. More like street-theatre than a religious ceremony. A welcome from the Dean was followed by hymns and prayers, the sermon and Communion, some communicants holding their pets – a dog, a cat or a rabbit tucked under the arm, a tortoise on a cushion, a parrot on the shoulder. The dogs barked, the cats meowed and the parrot squawked. Only the tortoise never made a sound.

Now came the moment we'd all been waiting for. The great bronze doors swung open and the 'Procession of Animals Great and Small' began, each and every creature garlanded with fresh flowers - accompanied, I hasten to add, by forty-eight men, women and children in impeccably ironed red robes!

Huey, the camel, was in the lead, followed by a llama and then a zebu. Next came a small calf, a miniature horse and a pygmy goat, a pot-bellied pig and a python wrapped scarf-like around a man's neck. There was an African hedgehog, a black-footed penguin, a great horned owl and hissing roaches as well as a ferret and a fossil rock, a tarantula and a tawny frogmouth, cathedral worms, algae and an iguana.

They all behaved beautifully. No bolters, no fighters and perfect toilet training. After the blessing they made their way back up the aisle, posing outside on the steps of the cathedral where a middle-aged blonde in trainers peeping out from under her red robe, informed me that Cornelius, her six-year-old 'altered' pot-bellied pig, ' has his very own bedroom with a queen-sized bed'. Only in America……

CHAPTER EIGHT

2000s

So in love with Africa were we that, for my 70th birthday and Martin's 71st (both 5th October) in 2000, we treated one another to a trip to Zambia, kicking off with a flight up north to Ndola in the Copper Belt to visit the Chimfunshi Wildlife Orphanage and finishing up with a walking safari in the South Luangua Valley.

David and Sheila Siddle started the Chimfunshi Wildlife Orphanage, after they accepted a badly injured infant chimp from a game ranger on their farm and nursed it back to health. An engineer by trade, Dave designed all the enclosures and handling facilities at Chimfunshi and pioneered many of the systems used by zoos and sanctuaries around the world. And in 2000, the year we were there, they had just opened two 500-acre enclosures for their chimps, still the largest area ever set aside for captive primates, and the closest thing to a wild release Zambia had ever seen.

Over the last 30 years Chimfunshi has provided a safe refuge for the hundreds of orphaned, injured and mistreated chimps, including Toto, the chimp rescued from a circus in Chile while others have been found on airport luggage carousels, chained to the rooftops of African restaurants, taken from shoddy little zoos or kept in crates as pets.

Dave's day-job was cattle farming which paid for the rescued chimps – with a little bit of help from two charities, Tusk Trust and WSPA. In 2002 both Dave and Sheila were awarded MBEs by the Queen and we met up with them at The Royal Geographical Society here in London where Sheila gave the annual Tusk Trust lecture to a full house and rapturous applause. Sadly, Dave died on 30th June 2006 at the age of 78 and at the time of his death, Chimfunshi was home to 112 chimps, making it one of the largest primate sanctuaries in the world.

It was here at Chimfunshi in 2000 that I had come to meet my adopted chimp, six-year-old Thompson.

On our first evening before my official photo-op with Thompson we were watching TV with month-old Miracle, a baby chimp born here but rejected by her mum and therefore hand-reared by Sheila. Miracle wore a nappy and knickers with her name embroidered on the front. Sheila let me hold her and she grabbed my hands tightly, just like human babies, and rose up on her feet, jumping up and down on my thighs. She was adorable.

Far more so, to me, than the real thing. If I could have given birth to one of these, I might have thought about getting pregnant!

While watching Francis Wilson's weather report on Sky News after dinner, I couldn't resist saying that I didn't recognise him with his clothes on. He lives in Hampstead and I used to see him every day on the Heath running in shorts, brown and bare-chested, with his great big Akita, always on the lead.

Suddenly Sheila leapt up off the sofa and shouted 'Oh my God, Billie! She realised Martin had gone to the outside loo for a pee and hadn't come back.

Billie was a female five-year-old orphan hippo, born on the river running through the Siddles' property. Her mother had been shot and Dave found her abandoned and dehydrated and brought her back to the house. She was fed milk in a gigantic bottle, reclining in the swimming pool the Siddles had built for their kids (luckily now having flown the nest) in the day time and sleeping on the sofa at night till it broke under her enormous weight and she was persuaded to sleep outside. Hippos kill more people in Africa than any other animal – and Martin was out there alone, in the dark and with a hippo on the loose.

Sheila found him trapped in the loo with Billie's gigantic head wedged in the doorway. Unable to escape, he'd been shouting for help and banging on the wall for the past half-an-hour but with the TV on we hadn't heard his SOS.

Sheila lured Billie away with a bottle of milk while Martin made a hasty retreat back to the house. There was no door on this outside loo, and while having a pee Martin had suddenly felt hot breath blowing on to his backside. When he turned around to see what it was coming from he nearly had a heart attack – there was a hippo's nostrils and gigantic jaws inches away from his buttocks.

Next it was my turn for an encounter with the wildlife of Africa. Sheila and Dominic, one of the chimp keepers, escorted us out to Thompson's quarters. They called his housemates to come inside for their breakfast but slammed down the drop-door before Thompson could join them. 'I want my breakfast, and I want it now!' he protested and far from posing for a picture, he stood on his hands and beat the door with his feet.

I thought he was going to smash it in but, suddenly, he had a change of heart and took a running jump into my arms. Have you ever felt the weight of a six-year-old chimp? Three times the weight of a six-year-old child. Chimps are all muscle and feel as though they're made of lead. Unluckily, I was standing next to the electric fence, camera raised ready for the perfect shot. Thompson landed on me with such force I fell on to the fence and got a severe shock. I screamed. Thompson fled and that was the end of our photo-shoot.

Next day Dominic invited us to join him and the baby chimps for a walk through the woods. The chimps loved this because we carried them piggy-back style. We sat down under the shade of an acacia tree and gave them some treats. Martin had lace-up boots on ready for our walking safari. One of the chimps undid the lace of one of his boots and took it out. He then did something quite amazing. He licked the end, just like my mother did when trying to thread cotton through a needle, and tried to get it back into the eyelet which he managed to do. But somehow he just couldn't get to grips with tying a bow!

One morning a young man, who was doing voluntary work for Tusk Trust, supporters of Chimfunshi, drove us to the two spanking brand new enclosures. There were trees for them to climb and ponds for them to splash around in. If their previous lives had been hell they were certainly now in chimp heaven. Our young driver remarked that his mother was extremely worried about his being out here in Africa. When we asked why, he solemnly replied that his brother had been eaten by a lion. While camping, he had left his tent unzipped at night because of the heat, his bare feet protruding through the opening. We'd read about this freak fatality death in the newspapers back home only a year earlier. And here were we about to embark on a week in the bush, although not actually camping, there was to be little between us and the local wildlife, save for a wall of woven reeds.

It was time to take off for Mfue and our walking safari. We were met at the tiny landing strip by one of the staff and taken to our first bush-camp at Louie. Our hut, one of six, was made of reeds with a roll-up reed blind at the window. I say 'window' but there was no window-pane, just a square hole in the reed wall. The hut was topped by a thatched roof and furnished with all mod. cons. Two single beds with mosquito nets, a flush loo and shower outside, surrounded by a reed fence. These bush-camps are taken down at the end of each season and rebuilt at the beginning of the next one. In today's terms they're pop-ups!

Dinner was served al fresco and was the stuff Michelin-stars are made of. Off to bed to get some shut-eye before our early morning call at five for our first game-walk. Martin was dead to the world when I heard heavy breathing. I gingerly rolled up the reed blind and I nearly had a heart attack. I was eye-to-eye with a whopping great elephant, its eyelashes like big black tarantulas. Shaking, I tip-toed over to Martin's bed, lifted up the mosquito-net, whispering in his ear 'Don't scream but there's an elephant at the window and it's eating our roof'. We kept dead still, our hearts beating so hard, I thought it would hear us and simply lean on the reed wall and flatten us in our beds. What a way to go! No wonder we were warned not to keep fruit in our rooms.

When we got our wake-up call just before dawn, once again I peered through the window. Around the camp fire were a dozen or so planter's chairs with big striped cushions. Our jumbo was having such fun. He'd picked up a cushion and was twirling it around with his trunk, like a drum majorette might do with a baton. When I opened the door of our hut, bushy tailed and bright eyed for our first walk on the wild side, right outside was a huge, round footprint, the size of a soup-plate. Luckily our jumbo had taken off!

After a mug of strong black tea, our guides, Radio and Deluxe, joined us for our walk in the bush. We had a guide with binox (as binoculars are called out here) and a gun leading us and another guide with a gun taking up the rear. There were two other couples with us and the six of us were told to walk single file, Indian style, and not to talk and to keep very, very quiet. One of the men was Southern Rhodesian/Zimbabwean who he greeted us wearing a T-shirt with the words 'FUCK THE RHINO, SAVE THE WHITES!'

Radio led us down an embankment into a dry sandy river-bed. The cliff edge was perforated with holes, the burrows of Carbine bee-eaters. These crimson birds (so called because of their ecclesiastical colours) were either taking off in search of prey, or landing with their beaks their stuffed full with flies. There were also murmurations (how I love that descriptions) of tiny little quelias which, up close were a brilliant shade of emerald green but en masse looked like fast moving clouds of grey smoke. Swaying this way and that they moved as one, seemingly never crashing into one another.

We could see all sorts of footprints in the sand, the spoor of different species going about their nocturnal business – hunting or being hunted. Death for herbivores is a nightly occurrence in the bush.

We walked along for half a mile and then climbed up out of the river-bed and on to a plateau where the grass was a high as an elephant's eye. Well, a lion's eye, as I was soon to find out. Although I wore long trousers and a long sleeved shirt, the tsetse flies were everywhere and extremely vicious, stabbing you through your clothing. Surrounded by the tall grass, I suddenly let out a piercing scream as one stabbed me through my shirtsleeve. Quick as a flash a male lion leapt up in the air just feet away and fled for dear life.

We walked to two more pop-up bush camps, our luggage going on ahead in the truck but there no more encounters of the wild kind, although we did have wonderful close sightings of elephant, lion, buffalo, hippo, wart-hog and, most exciting of all because they are so rare, a pack of wild dogs lying at the bottom of the bank on the edge of the sandy river bed. So as not frighten them away, we stood rock still, slowly raising our binoculars. They really are cartoon characters with their great long legs, big fluffy ears, deep chicken-chests and beautiful mottled coats, nature's perfect camouflage.

Soon after getting home from our walking safari in Zambia, perhaps still in thrall to the wild dogs we'd chanced upon, Martin suddenly announced 'If we're ever going to have another dog, it'd better be before we get any older'. He was right. We had just hit our seventies and there weren't that many years left when we'd be up and running to take on a dog. 'Why don't you give Anne a ring to see if she's got any 'galgos' coming out of quarantine', he added.

The previous year, while walking on the Heath, we had stopped to speak to a woman with a long flowing chestnut mane, and three greyhounds. She turned out to be actress Charlotte Cornwell (David Cornwell's sister, aka author John le Carré) who ran the charity 'Greyhounds UK' with fellow actress Annette Crosbie of 'One Foot in the Grave' fame. She told us about the plight of racers here in the UK with some 7,000 being dumped every year from the tracks at just four years old. A mere 3,000 are ever rehomed. The rest just disappear while in Spain ex-hunters, known as 'galgos', are hanged by the neck with wire in the olive groves, their owners not wanting to feed them till the next hunting season.

Shortly after our encounter with Charlotte Cornwell, a friend sent me a cutting from The Mirror about a nurse, Anne Finch, who, with her husband Arthur, had founded a charity called Greyhounds in Need in 1998, its mission being the welfare and rescue of greyhounds, especially those in Spain. We decided, there and then, that if ever we had another dog, it would certainly be a greyhound, and, probably, a 'galgo'; the native greyhounds of Spain.

And so I rang Anne Finch asking if she had any galgos coming out of quarantine any time soon. 'Three on Thursday', she replied. That focused the mind but before hot-footing it up to the quarantine kennels in Nottingham we had to find out whether each and every one was cat friendly because we had two, Queenie and Kodak. 'I'll test all three on our cat, Lucky', the woman in charge of the kennels kindly volunteered, later ringing to say Lucky was still Lucky!

We left early to get first choice from Pip, Squeak and Wilfred – a brindle, a black and a black-and-white. All three of them came rushing up to greet us. Martin turned around to me, saying 'It's the brindle job or nothing!' And so the brindle it was. Pip was quite exquisite. We'd had dogs of all breeds during our forty years of marriage but never one of these daddy-longlegs. Our love affair with greyhounds was just beginning.

These Spanish greyhounds are the progeny of the original sighthounds used all over the Middle East for hunting. They are designer dogs with beautiful long heads, long giraffe-like necks and tails so long they barely skim the ground. They don't bite, they don't bark, they don't smell, they don't fight and they are drip dry.

It's sad to think that with all these virtues they are one of the most abused breeds in the world. In medieval times, only noblemen were allowed to own these elegant creatures but over the years they've sunk to the bottom of the heap owing to the so-called 'sport' of greyhound racing and other abusive treatment, including their use for hunting in Spain.

We signed the adoption papers on the spot and changed his name from Pip to Harry, deciding that Pip was totally inappropriate for such a noble creature.

Harry jumped onto the back seat of our car and never looked back, driving south to his new life in leafy Hampstead, having spent the last six months incarcerated in a kennel with just a small concrete run. Little did he know that eight hundred acres of Hampstead Heath awaited him.

That was on the 4th of December 2000 and the next six and a half years were a wonderful experience, owning one of these very special dogs. To watch Harry running on Hampstead Heath was a show-stopper. He just flew through the air like a cheetah. We also basked in reflected glory when people remarked 'what a beautiful dog' which they did every time he set foot outside our front door.

A decade previously you would never have seen a greyhound, let alone a 'galgo', on Hampstead Heath as a pet but at last people are discovering that these hounds don't need hours and hours of exercise. They run for the sheer joy of running when out but, once home, become couch potatoes. They are not like terriers, as we well know, which never leave you alone, demanding little dogs that they are.

As we went out on our morning walks with Harry I began to see more and more of these designer dogs. Within months I knew sixteen ex-racers, which came from either the Retired Greyhound Trust or Battersea Dogs' Home, as well as a dozen or so' lurchers' – a greyhound cross. But back then there was only one 'galgo' and that was our boy, Harry.

The following summer I decided to hold a greyhound gathering on the Heath on The Pasture Ground, a big grassy open-space directly below Kenwood House. At 3 pm. sharp on a sunny Sunday afternoon, greyhounds began to appear from all directions. Within half an hour there were thirty-two: brindles and beiges, blacks, whites and even a blue called Blue. This being Hampstead, they answered to Freud, Norton, Casper, Oslo, Oscar, Jack and Jerry, Mercedes, Molly and Miranda. But shouting out almost any one of these names around here it could just as easily have been be a child that came running.

The purpose of our greyhound gathering was twofold: to encourage people to adopt these gentle giants, by highlighting their plight when their racing or hunting days are over, and to introduce Harry to Miranda.

Harry, our dog, a handsome brindle 'galgo' was rescued from Spain by the British charity, Greyhounds in Need. Traditionally, at the end of each four-month season, the owners hang them by the neck with wire from trees. By disposing of their dogs in this brutal manner, they are saved the price of a bullet as well as the cost of feeding them until the next season. They then get new ones at the beginning of the next hunting season and this cycle of cruelty begins all over again.

Miranda, a brindle bitch, was also rescued, but from closer to home. At four years old she was retired from Walthamstow Stadium and re-homed by the Retired Greyhound Trust. Although some 9,000 racing greyhounds are retired every year from British tracks alone, only a small proportion are ever re-homed. The Trust found homes for more than 2,000 last year, but with well over 20,000 being bred every year in Ireland, those surplus to worldwide requirements run into thousands.

Having got lost on Hampstead Heath while chasing a squirrel, Miranda was currently the local canine celebrity. Hundreds of posters bearing her picture had been put up and, because Harry looked so much like her, I was asked daily whether he was Miranda. Two weeks later her owners, Edward and Sandrine Foster, were rung up early one morning by a builder who had found her starving and collapsed on his site, 20 miles away, in Hatfield.

He gave her water and the pork sausages he was going to cook for his lunch and managed to get close enough to read the telephone number on her identity disc. The relieved and jubilant Fosters rushed out to Hatfield to collect her and found a very skinny, footsore and weary dog.

She had lost 30% of her body weight, her pads were raw, her nails worn down and she had an injured eye – probably caused by having been hit by a car. She was completely dehydrated and the vet put her on a drip, her kidneys about to go into meltdown. The story made the front page of our local paper. She subsequently put back on most of her weight but, sadly, lost the sight in her left eye.

Like all stars, Miranda was the last to arrive at our gathering. There were cheers when she finally appeared, her arrival coinciding with that of our other star of the day, television presenter Katie Boyle, who was a trustee of Battersea Dogs Home and a greyhound-lover. Katie said: 'They make such perfect pets for young and old alike, being quiet, calm, affectionate and obedient. And, no, they do not need hours of exercise. They are actually couch potatoes.'

When Harry met Miranda, there was much tail wagging. Would they become an item? I fear not, since they had both been 'altered', as the Americans say. 'They're just good friends', laughed Katie.

When we'd had Harry for about eighteen months he became ill. After several tests our vet remembered he'd come from Spain and suggested that it might be leishmania and his blood samples were sent to both Bristol and Liverpool University Vet Schools. Liverpool, which deals with the human variant, declared its test positive. By then Harry was skeletal, his hair falling out and he could hardly stand. We took him to the vet to have him put down but he suggested that we should try the drug of choice for this disease – Allopurinal, prescribed for gout. Harry spent a week on a drip with daily doses of this drug. It worked like magic and within three months he'd made a complete recovery but had to stay on the drug for the rest of his life.

Leishmania is a disease largely unknown in this country, except to owners of dogs imported from southern Europe and well-informed vets. It can only be contracted by dogs bitten by a sandfly, which has already bitten an infected animal. It has similarities to human malaria, being a virulent fever which is repetitive, incurable, but fairly easily treated. Dogs on long-term medication often lead normal active lives but have their life spans shortened, often markedly so.

Five years after his recovery Harry tore a ligament while running on The West Meadow on Hampstead Heath, swerving to avoid hitting a tree. We tried rest, acupuncture, physiotherapy and hydrotherapy but nothing worked. Finally, we resorted to surgery at The Royal Veterinary College but after a couple of months recuperating, his back became twisted and he was unable to walk. A scan showed that scar tissue was pressing on his spinal-chord and his condition was pronounced untreatable. While sleeping off the anaesthetic after the scan, we asked the RVC to put him down. I cried all day and every day.

My husband suggested we rang GIN's rehoming officer to see if there were any galgos due for release from quarantine that weren't spoken for. The good news was that there was just one, a brindle male, due out in two months' time. The bad news was that he was a very traumatised animal, having been abandoned at the end of the hunting season in Spain and was found injured. Starving, he'd tried to eat the bait in a fox trap and had got caught. We rushed up to the kennels to take a look at Niko and couldn't believe our eyes – he was Harry's double. He looked so sad, so how could we possibly not say we'd have him?

During those two months we had time to grieve for Harry but also to look forward to welcoming our new dog. I'd had a great uncle Harry, whose brother, Percy, was my grandfather and so we decided to keep it in the family and call him Percy.

So alike did Harry and Percy look that our local newsagent, who greeted Harry every morning when Martin went to get the papers and didn't know that we'd got a new dog, on seeing Percy for the very first time kindly remarked 'Your dog is looking so much better now'!

Although identical to look at, they couldn't have been more different in their behaviour. Chalk and cheese. Fillet steak and Pedigree Chum. Whereas Harry was friendly from day one, Percy was petrified of everything and everyone. This was not too surprising, given his history. We had to turn our backs towards him when walking past his basket. Eye contact terrified him. He wasn't housetrained, probably having been kept in a shed on a farm, had never been walked on a lead and obviously had never been stroked. If we put out a hand to pat him he thought he was about to be attacked, leaping out of his basket to hide in the corner.

It took nine months of tender, loving care as well as the help and advice of two dog trainers to get Percy to respond to us. He was so depressed that he hung his head as though in shame, while his extraordinarily long tail never wagged, hanging down like a piece of dead meat. A friend wanted to know if he was affectionate at home and when I replied 'No', asked if I regretted having taken him on. I said he needed a home and we needed a dog.

Strangely for such a nervous dog, he didn't bat an eyelid at loud noises or fireworks, whereas the calm and collected Harry would crouch in a corner, shivering every year for the entire month of November when fireworks would begin and end two weeks either side of the 5th, our quiet little neighbourhood seemingly turned into a war-zone.

Gradually, we began to see signs of improvement in Percy, helped by hand feeding to gain his trust. He enjoyed having his back rubbed and started to go into play-mode with the squeaky toy tiger, given to Harry but which he totally ignored. He never gave it a second glance after a friend presented it to him. Percy adores it and every morning while I am changing into my walking boots, he rushes up and down the kitchen excitedly throwing it up into the air or gently biting it to make it growl. One day he threw it into his water bowl and it nearly drowned!

Within a year I could truly say he was morphing into Harry and becoming a loving and happy dog. Meanwhile, my husband, who had become a trustee of GIN while we had Harry, was suddenly thrust into becoming Chairman as Anne Finch retired due to ill health and her husband, Arthur, had died of cancer.

One summer's evening I took him out for a pee round the crescent opposite to our house. Halfway round a huge dog, a Portuguese Mountain Dog, the size and colour of a lion, jumped over a low garden wall, pinned Percy to a parked car and sank its teeth into his belly.

The reason greyhounds wear those funny crescent shaped collars is because their narrow heads, which are no wider than their necks, make it easy for them to slip a collar. We always made sure that while out on the Heath Percy's collar was quite tight, releasing it a notch when we got home. Luckily that evening I hadn't tightened it, which probably saved his life. While I was screaming at the owner to pull her dog off, Percy cleverly slipped his collar and ran for his life and by the time I got back home he was waiting for me at the front door.

He jumped straight into his basket and looked OK but later I noticed he had a bloody, red hole on the soft tissue just below his ribcage where the lion had sunk its fangs into him. By then our vet surgery was closed so we rushed him to an emergency vet where he had to be stitched up, spending the night there. When we collected him the next morning we were presented with a bill for £721. Since I knew very well where the owner lived, I presented it to her and she reimbursed us on the spot. Nevertheless we were left nursing an injured and traumatised animal.

In a decade from knowing absolutely nothing about the plight of greyhounds, we had been thrown in at the deep end. Here was my husband at the age of 80, supposedly retired, working harder than ever rescuing these magnificent creatures from a fate worse than death in Spain but, like every other greyhound owner, enjoying every minute in the company of such wonderful, elegant looking and lovable dogs. I've never met an owner who hasn't confided 'I'll never have any other breed'.

GIN was founded by Anne and Arthur Finch in 1998 with the objective of rescuing, treating and rehoming galgos, the native hunting greyhounds of Spain. Anne had discovered the appalling plight of these dogs which are used for hunting and coursing in the rural parts of Spain, mainly the south. After a hunting season of only four months these beautiful hounds are routinely destroyed by the most brutal methods or simply abandoned to their fate in cruelly hot and barren conditions.

Anne Finch describes how she got started:

'As long ago as the 1980s I became aware of the crying needs of hundreds of unwanted greyhounds. Greyhound racing started as a gambling sport in the 1930s and they soon started filling up rescue kennels as they were often abandoned while still very young.

'My concern deepened when I learned of the export from Ireland of low-grade greyhounds abroad. They were sold at £50 each to four tracks in Spain.. An amateur video made in 1990 showed the harsh conditions of the kennels in Barcelona where over 1000 Irish greyhounds were cooped up in metre-square cages piled on top of each other, many with untreated wounds and fractures, and with diseases such as distemper. All were unvaccinated and without any veterinary care.

'Who was going to do anything about it? It seemed it was up to me and my husband Arthur to alleviate their plight. In 1991, I explored the possibilities for rescuing dogs in Spain but it was difficult because of quarantine and airline regulations. I explained my cause to British Airways and they offered free flight places for three dogs from Barcelona. Then two Kennels offered free quarantine places. I was now up to my neck in it whether I liked it or not and had to seize the chance. I had never been to Spain before and knew no Spanish. For six weeks I worked out details of the operation, barely sleeping, and still had to carry on with my full time nursing job.

'I flew back with four pathetic-looking ear-marked Irish greyhounds and took them to a specialist greyhound racing vet who found unhealed and untreated fractures, malnourishment, skin disease and tropical disease from embedded ticks, fleas and other parasites.

'I reported back to the World Greyhound Racing Federation, which undertook an official inspection of racing kennels in Spain. Gradually conditions improved and in 1994, I embarked on an instructional video in Spanish. It took two years to produce but spelt

153

out the conditions under which a racing dog had to be treated. There was no longer any excuse for ignorance.

'In time, all four Spanish tracks closed down, which meant finding homes and solutions for hundreds of needy greyhounds. I shared my material with TV companies in Germany, Switzerland, Holland, France and Belgium in the hope that dog devotees abroad would extend their sympathies to the greyhound and offer help. It took years of perseverance, many visits, and many walks down blind alleys. At the time, it was all being paid for out of my nursing salary but gradually some real stars emerged who were willing to share this burden with me in Spain.

'We had to beg for manpower, money, veterinary care, vehicles and drivers and finally, loving homes for these needy dogs. Nothing was easy.

'Back home, disquiet among those of us involved in greyhound rescue was accelerating and in 1994 there was a large meeting in London chaired by the RSPCA and Dogs' Trust and attended by the sporting press, racing associations and those burdened with the fallout from greyhound racing. It was an angry meeting but out of it came the Greyhound Forum, where those involved both in racing and rehoming greyhounds could come together.

'Meanwhile I was becoming aware of a second need in Spain, that of the 'galgos', Spain's own breed of greyhound. In 1995 in Madrid I was shown a video of the hanging of 'galgos' at the end of their four-month hunting season each year. In two years, we transported nearly 200 of these dogs to homes abroad. Donations now started to come in and we became registered in 1998 as the charity Greyhounds in Need.'

Here, Martin, Chairman of Trustees, explains his involvement with Greyhounds in Need. Our Patrons are well known dog lover Jilly Cooper, who has herself rehomed several rescue dogs, and actor Peter Egan who currently has a pack of six. And , of course, the late Alexandra Bastedo.

'While there are many charities in the UK helping to home Irish and UK greyhounds, only GIN concentrates its efforts in Spain. GIN has been instrumental in rescuing and rehoming well over 6,000 'galgos' and the work continues as the close of each hunting season sees the abandonment, or worse, of hundreds of these abused animals.

'My own involvement began when, after Angela and I had first adopted a 'galgo' from GIN, Anne Finch asked me to be a Trustee. She said, 'Martin, we'd love you to become a Trustee; don't worry, it only involves three meetings a year. ' Being a sucker for punishment and by that time besotted with greyhounds, I agreed. It wasn't long before poor Arthur and Anne were forced by ill health to retire. So I suddenly became the Chairman of Trustees, while still crawling up a steep learning curve and only saved by a superb General Manager from floundering out of my depth.

'With the help of a truly wonderful band of supporters, GIN continues to expand its vital work. As I write, (2014) we have recently completed the construction of a new range of kenneling for 'galgos', complete with proper weather protection and underfloor heating at a rescue centre in Albacete in Southern Spain. Our next project is to supply and equip a new van for the transport of the dogs we home in other European countries. Meanwhile the work of veterinary care and homing continues.

'Only last year we heard of several galgos, some just puppies, left to starve to death in a cave, tied by their necks to heavy rocks. On my last visit to Spain I was shown a new arrival which had had a rear foot cut off by its hunter owner as a form of "punishment". Although these are some of the extreme cases, all these hunting greyhounds are subjected to cruelty and neglect, before being abandoned, or worse, savagely killed.

'This cause has largely taken over my life, but at the same time it has given me huge satisfaction and an appreciation of the wonderful qualities of these long suffering creatures and of the heroic efforts by many Spaniards and other caring people to rescue and rehome them.

Looking to the future, we have embarked on the difficult task of trying to educate the younger generation in rural Spain to respect all animals and particularly their wonderful 'galgos'. There lies the only hope of salvation for the dogs we so love and respect.'

In 2002, on one of my last writing trips, I was very close to one of Africa's big cats. Schmoozle, a young male cheetah, was sitting facing us on the bonnet of our Land Rover, his tear-stained cheeks, huge golden eyes and bloody jaws just feet away.

Andy, our driver-cum-guide, was hand-feeding big chunks of raw, red meat to this exquisite creature.

I had heard of the work of the AfriCat Foundation in Namibia with leopards, lions and, in particular, with cheetahs and wanted to see it for myself. After all, it is not every day that you can look straight into the eyes of one of Africa's large carnivores in its natural habitat on a warm, balmy evening. This was pure animal magic.

The world's fastest mammals, cheetahs are able to run at 68mph. They achieve this enormous speed using their long legs and a supple spine which lets them fold up then explode in acceleration. Such speed is short-lived and takes all their energy, but it enables them to catch their prey. In this, cheetahs are much like greyhounds, built in a similar way. In some safari parks, cheetahs are given a daily cheetah run, where they chase a mechanical rabbit in much the same way as a greyhound. If they do not get their daily run, they become depressed and miserable.

One thing you learn working with many animal species, is how very different they all are. Some are solitary, some are herd animals, some are friendly and some are hostile. Some animals, such as elephants and lions, are very intelligent while others, like sheep are quite stupid. Yet in today's world so many cannot live out their natural instincts or express their natural personalities.

Namibia is four times the size of Britain and twice the size of France, but its population is just under two million. However, although it is sparsely populated, it has the largest concentration of cheetahs in Africa, with 90% living on livestock farmland. Not surprisingly, this generates conflict with humans who are the greatest threat to the species. The survival of the cheetahs now lies with 1,000 or so commercial farmers, who can kill them legally. Being considered vermin, some 10,000 have been caught in box-traps, leg-hold traps, poisoned or simply shot on sight over the past two decades.

But not only are cheetahs hunted by farmers, they are at risk, too, from marauding lions, loss of habitat and a reduced gene pool – and so their very survival hangs in the balance.

The AfriCat Foundation, a non-profit-making organisation, was trying to halt the destruction of this endangered species through farmer assistance, youth education, research and encouraging animal welfare.

Many farmers did not want to kill the predators once they'd caught them, so they were now able to contact AfriCat who will collect them, give them a health check and keep them in their holding facilities for veterinary treatment or relocation to a private game reserve. Old and sick predators that were unfit to be returned to the wild are either put down or looked after in large enclosures at the AfriCat Foundation.

Back in 1970, when the Hanssen family purchased Okonjima Farm, 30 miles south of Otjiwarongo, in the north of Namibia, to breed Brahmin cattle. Life became a struggle, though, when carnivores, particularly leopards, caused extensive losses among their herd. After having little or no success with common forms of predator removal, they developed techniques to protect their livestock and dramatically reduced the problem.

Slowly, because of its convenient location between Windhoek, Namibia's capital city in the central highlands, and Etosha, one of Africa's great national parks, and also because of the abundant birdlife there, Okonjima began to get involved in tourism. At the same time, the farm became known as a place for animal welfare because of the successful rearing of Chinga, a young cheetah cub, and farmers contacted the Hanssens to obtain advice and help with their own predator problems.

The need for a foundation that could offer assistance and develop further solutions soon became clear so, in 1993, the AfriCat Foundation was formally established and the Hanssens switched completely from cattle farming to tourism. Today, although the AfriCat Foundation and Okonjima Lodge share Okonjima Farm, the two are separate, but have, in fact, a mutually beneficial relationship.

We were staying at Okonjima Bush Camp. This brand new luxury lodge is hardly my idea of roughing it – it comprises half-a-dozen or so thatched rondavels, with all mod. cons. in the form of hot showers, flush loos and big comfy beds, as well as an open-sided main building for gourmet wining and dining. The profits from the camp go towards supporting the big cats which have been trapped for relocation or can never be returned to the wild, - hence our close encounter with a cheetah on the bonnet.

On our first afternoon's game-drive with Andy, he spotted a leopard lying in the branches of a tree, keeping watch over its dinner from on high. Down below, and already swarming with flies, was the body of a young kudu buck, killed earlier in the day. Crouching nearby was the leopard's mate and their two 18-month-old cubs. The parents had been brought up as pets and, when the owners could no longer cope, they were given to AfriCat where they were taught to fend for themselves and successfully put back into the wild.

While we were at Okonjima there were as many as 73 cheetahs in large holding pens waiting to be transferred to areas where they would not prey on farmers' livestock. Another nine were living in a 50-acre enclosure as, having been injured or orphaned, they were unable to hunt and had to be fed.

I adopted one of these, four-year-old Hadar who, with his siblings Hector, Hercules and Portia, came to AfriCat when they were just six months old. Their mother was shot by a farmer, who claimed not to have noticed that she had cubs at the time.

A pair of youngsters, Tyke and his sister, Spike, were hit by a car while following their mother across a road and, luckily, the driver took them to a vet. Spike's leg was pinned and she was taken to AfriCat but Tyke's leg was shattered. While the vet was deciding whether to put him down or amputate the leg, Spike began to pine for her brother. So, to save her life, it was decided that Tyke's leg should be amputated and today, eight years later, brother and sister are inseparable.

I mentioned to Andy when we said our goodbyes that these lovely cats reminded us so much of our exquisite dog, Harry. He said that the greyhound was in many ways in similar body conformation to the cheetah – very long legs for speed, a long and supple spine as well as long toes for easy twisting and turning when hunting, and big deep chicken-like chests to house their huge lungs.

A big event was looming, at least for Martin and myself: our 50th wedding anniversary. Here we were, about to become an endangered species ourselves, having stayed together for half a century when many of our contemporaries were on spouses number two, three, or even four!

Since becoming supporters of Jill Robinson's charity Animals Asia in 2003, we had longed to go to Chengdu to see for ourselves the sanctuary of rescued Moon Bears. As luck would have it, a Bale's brochure plopped through the letter-box featuring its long-haul destinations around the world, including China. There was one itinerary which fitted the bill perfectly, taking in the highlights of this vast country with an option of a two-day side trip to Chengdu, which included our actual anniversary, to see the pandas. 'To hell with the pandas', we cried 'they get all the attention, we want to see the Moon Bears which suffer in silence and get none'.

Our late afternoon flight to Chengdu was delayed for four hours but the lovely Jill was there to meet and greet us as the clock struck midnight, ushering in the 21st of April, our big day. After breakfast Jill took us around the sanctuary, our first stop being to take pictures of the huge stack of rusty iron cages in which these magnificent beasts had been incarcerated for up to thirty years. Thirty years without being able to move! They were quite unable to escape the metal catheter thrust into their gall-bladders with no anaesthetic from which they were milked for bile every single day of their painful lives. Man's inhumanity to man is hard enough to comprehend but man's inhumanity to animals knows no boundaries.

From the 'cages of shame' it was heart-warming to see those bears lucky enough to have been rescued, lounging around on purpose-built platforms, lazing in hammocks, climbing trees or, even better, splashing about in their own private pools. They'd gone from Bear Hell to Bear Heaven.

That evening Jill put Rupert, the blind bear to bed, closing the door between his night and day quarters. She gave us some blue plastic overshoes, so as not to spread infection, and invited us into Rupert's little garden. Because of his disability he had his own private quarters where we sat, knocking back the bottle of bubbly Jill had so kindly bought for us. What a wonderful way to celebrate not only our 50th but also the freedom of these poor bears.

In 2013, it was Jill's turn to celebrate – the twentieth anniversary of the founding of Animals Asia. So much has happened in those twenty years, with more and more Chinese people coming on side and the charity growing to become an international player in animal welfare in the Far East. Not only does it work to close down the bile farms but is also tackling the dog and cat-meat trade in which these domestic pets suffer a horrendous death.

Jill Robinson tells the story of how she was inspired to found Animals Asia:

'My world changed in April 1993 when I walked into a bear farm in China. I was living in Hong Kong with my husband John and was already involved in animal welfare, trying to find solutions to the live animal markets in China and dog and cat markets of the Philippines and South Korea, where they were bludgeoned to death or drowned in boiling water, but this was something else.

'One female bear stretched out her paw in a gesture of help and from then on, I knew there was no way of going back to an ordinary life. This animal was one of some 10,000 Asiatic black bears, often known as Moon Bears after the yellow crescent of fur on their chests, which were kept for their bile.

'Surgically mutilated and with a catalogue of injuries and wounds that would fill a hall of shame, these bears were caged for decades so that their body fluid can be used in Chinese traditional medicine, despite the fact that cheap and readily available herbs and synthetic bile had existed for many years.

'I gave the bear which had stretched out her paw the name of Hong, let her gently squeeze my fingers and promised myself that her suffering would never been in vain and that she would represent a species that somehow, one day, could be saved from their tortured lives on the farms.

'Today, while I am sure that the actual Hong is long dead, she is with me still – in a tattoo on my shoulder. Her image represents the campaign of Animals Asia. Starting and running a foundation has not been easy, but I was given a great deal of help by my friend and mentor, Virginia McKenna. She said, 'just do it' and her encouragement sealed my future.

'I began Animals Asia in a room of my house, with a remit to end bear farming and the human consumption of dogs and cats.

'Today, we have award-winning bear sanctuaries in China and Vietnam which house 400 rescued bears, and three flagship programmes: Ending Bear Bile Farming, Cat and Dog Welfare, and Zoos and Safari Parks, but the bile bears remain our priority.

'The suffering of these majestic, forgiving animals is beyond comprehension, and such is the extent of damage from the crude surgery they undergo, that every farmed and extracted bear in China requires the removal of their chronically inflamed and infected gall bladders. The bears are also often deliberately abused by having their teeth cut back to gum level, exposing pulp and nerves, and their paw tips hacked away to stop the claws from growing. Many of the bears even grow into the bars of the cages which hold them immobile for anything up to 30 years; their natural lifespan.

'They suffer psychologically too, and have open wounds and scars on their heads from where they have smashed their foreheads against the bars of the cage. They will often also chew on the bars of the cage, breaking their own teeth.

'Nowadays, the majority of people in China are against this barbaric and unnecessary industry. In 2012, the practice of bile bear farming was officially one of the top ten discussion points in China's parliament and we are seeing support at all levels of the media. We also have the support of many celebrities, including actress Rula Lenska, Olivia Newton John, Stephen Fry, Peter Egan, comedian Ricky Gervais and his partner, author, Jane Fallon'.

Our own adopted bear, Oliver, nicknamed the 'broken bear' because he suffered in a cage for 30 years of his life. Tired and worn out, yet with a joyous enthusiasm for food, sun, grass and life, Oliver is the perfect ambassador for his species, showing just how brave and stoic they are.

Here is Oliver's own heartwarming story, told in diary format:

'In April 2010, the Animals Asia team rescued 10 tortured bears from the dilapidated buildings of a bear farm in Shandong in the north of China. The rescue and return journey to Chengdu, a distance of over 2,000km or more than 1,300 miles, took four long days.

Monday 19 April

Inside the farm building, in rusting, dangerous cages of various sizes were six moon bears and four brown bears, all staring out with dull eyes, anxious and in pain.

In an old, rusty cage with the ceiling above him on the verge of collapse was Oliver, a majestic brown bear with short, squat limbs. He appeared unresponsive and in pain. The farmer admitted that Oliver had spent a total of 30 years caged on farms, suffering the torture of bile extraction and confined in a painful, heavy metal jacket.

Oliver's condition caused concern among the rescue team from the beginning. But because of the position of the cages, he was the last bear to be removed from the farm.

Finally anaesthetised and removed from his cage, Oliver was given his first health-check. As the night drew in and the rain fell, the vet team made him as comfortable as they could for the long journey home to Chengdu.

Tuesday 20 April

The first day on the road passed without incident, but Oliver's reluctance to eat or drink had begun to cause concern, along with the fact that the convoy had come to a virtual standstill in a huge traffic jam.

Wednesday 21 April

As the second day on the road dawned, Oliver's condition had deteriorated so badly that emergency surgery was needed to save his life. With the help of local traffic police, his truck was rushed through to a nearby hospital that had agreed to offer assistance. The vet team prepared for surgery as the hospital staff set up oxygen and lighting.

Under extreme conditions, with rain streaming down and the temperature outside dropping, Oliver underwent a four-hour operation in the back of the truck to remove his damaged gall bladder.

Embedded in the tissue of his gall bladder was a crude metal ring with a hook that had protruded through his abdomen for years to extract the bile, causing infection and incredible pain.

Thursday 22 April

The next day broke sunny and warm and Oliver woke with an

appetite, eating watermelon and pineapple and drinking water for the first time since his rescue. It was a good sign for the rest of the journey.

Friday 23 April

After four days on the road, the team arrived back at the rescue centre in the early hours of Friday where Oliver was finally settled into hospital to await a second round of surgery.

The road to recovery.

Recovering well from his ordeal and surgeries, Oliver was quickly moved into his own den to give him his first taste of freedom. With joy written all over his face, Oliver couldn't move fast enough to explore his new space. Curious and excited, he searched the den for hidden treats and played with anything he could get his paws on.

As soon as Oliver had built up his strength, the doors to his outdoor enclosure were opened. Free at last, he relishes everything about his new home, foraging and dashing about as fast as his elderly body allows.

One encouraging sign is that over 1,000 pharmacies in China have now pledged not to sell or prescribe bile bear products.'

It was back to Africa yet again in late 2009 for a double celebration. Virginia McKenna was accompanying a small group to Kenya to celebrate The Born Free Foundation's 25th anniversary. As I'd become a supporter from the very beginning when the charity was known as Zoo Check, how could we miss such an opportunity to celebrate with its film star founder?

It was also Martin's 80th (and my 79[th)] on 5th October so we splashed out and joined the group in Nairobi. Our first stop was none other than Daphne Sheldrick's Elephant Orphanage where we met up with Virginia. It was some fourteen years since we were last there to meet my adopted Emily, now rehabilitated into the wild at Tsavo National Park and mother of her own calf.

It was then on to Elsa's Kopje where Joy and George had hand reared their famous orphan lion cub, which not only became the star of the best seller, 'Born Free', but a real-life film star, too. We had a gala dinner that night in the beautiful open-sided lodge, after which there was a private viewing of the famous film of that name where Virginia and Bill played Joy and George.

The following morning we had a celebratory brunch, which had been set up by the staff ahead of us, in a clearing surrounded by trees close to Elsa's grave. We all raised our glasses to the long deceased Joy, George and Elsa and, of course, Virginia's beloved husband Bill – all four doing so much to highlight the plight of these majestic beasts. And, to Virginia for having founded Born Free, along with Bill, twenty five years earlier which still continues the fight to KEEP WILDLIFE IN THE WILD. And to my husband, Martin, too, just for having made eighty!

Every Thursday we buy our local newspaper, The Hampstead & Highgate Express, known as The Ham & High. On the morning of 24th of April, 2008, while eating my boiled egg, the headlines on Page 2 well and truly grabbed my eye. 'JOEY ON WAY TO RECOVERY AFTER YEARS OF MISERY – monkey rescued from abuse in Hampstead house is making good progress at sanctuary'. And there were two pictures – one of two capuchins taken at The Monkey Sanctuary at Looe in Cornwall and the other of the cage in which Joey had spent many cramped years.

I read on. 'A monkey abandoned in Hampstead and left deformed after a decade of abuse is now making a miraculous recovery. Joey, a black-capped capuchin, was left with brittle bones, a paralysed face and severe mental problems after being locked inside a tiny cage at a home in …….. .' Our very road – a wide leafy street in respectable Hampstead Village. We know many of the residents and could never have imagined that a neighbour had been keeping a monkey here in a cage for <u>nine years</u>!

I immediately rang the Sanctuary to find out what number Joey had been rescued from but because the RSPCA had collected him, they didn't know the number of the house. However, we decided not only to 'adopt' (sponsor) him but made a date for the following November to go and meet our erstwhile neighbour.

Apparently, the woman owner and her man-friend had bought Joey in a market in Surinam in South America. After a decade the owner returned to South America leaving her friend to come in to feed Joey every day and apart from his visits Joey was left was in solitary confinement where he never saw sunlight and his only company was a tiny television, left on night and day but with the sound switched off. 'You know when an animal starts rocking back and forth it is in distress' he said and a year later when the owner had failed to return he called the RSPCA which took Joey down to The Monkey Sanctuary Trust in Cornwall.

Then a strange coincidence happened. While walking my then greyhound, Harry, on Hampstead Heath I met a friend. I'd already told her about Joey and so she asked if I'd seen the story in that week's Sunday Times Magazine 'THE EVIL CAREER OF THE BAD SAMARITAN' by Tim Rayment. I hadn't and she kindly popped it through my letterbox the following day.

This whole saga got weirder and weirder. The story was about one Vanessa Campbell ,'born Maryan Lesley Persaud in Georgetown, Guyana, a woman with a light Indian skin and impeccable clothes who made millions by convincing rich, even famous, people that they would become ill or die if they didn't give her money'. Not only had she defrauded people out of thousands but had rented four flats, an entire house, at a cost of £8,000 a month in none other than our very street in Hampstead, living there alone with a capuchin monkey she had bought in a market in Surinam as a guard-dog!

When Joey arrived in Cornwall he had not been outside for nine years nor had he seen another monkey since he was three months old – when he was taken from the wild as a baby to be sold in a market.

He had severe metabolic bone disease caused by an insufficient diet and lack of sunshine and exercise and would have been in constant pain.

Several pictures illustrated the story, and one was of the friend who had come in daily to feed and give some solace to the lonely Joey. I immediately recognised him as the man who parked his car nearby and would go up the steps into a house diagonally opposite ours. I felt like weeping. This poor little creature had been so near and yet so far and had endured a decade of a bad diet, lack of sunshine and exercise and, latterly, 22-hours a day of loneliness.

That November we made our way to The Monkey Sanctuary where staff members Katie Hobbs and Gill Maltby welcomed us. I already knew Gill because she also worked for Animals Asia Foundation.

Prior to actually meeting Joey we were shown his crate in which he was incarcerated for a decade while Gill told us his sad little story. Joey, is a black-capped Capuchin monkey (Cebus apella) and was born in the wild in Surinam in March 1998, arriving at The Sanctuary on 28th August, 2007, after nine years on his own in a 6 x 4 x2ft.cage. When found he was rocking backwards and forwards clutching a small blanket and his toy polar bear for comfort, having been regularly left for 22 hours a day, only visited by Vanessa Campbell's friend for two, while he fed him and cleaned his cage and gave him a cuddle.

Joey now spends his days enjoying his new home and life at the Sanctuary where he quickly made friends with the other monkeys, particularly Charlie Brown and Kodak. Joey and Kodak spend hours playing with one another and grooming each other. 'We were very worried about him when he first arrived' said Gill ' wondering whether he would be able to adapt to the massive change in his life but are delighted that he has shown himself to be so resilient, stealing the hearts of all those who meet him'.

And that's exactly what he did to his ex-neighbours, Angela and Martin Humphery. I cried. I begged him to forgive us for not having come to his rescue. If only we'd known he was but a stone's throw from us, suffering as he did for those nine years. We happily watched him scampering along the specially adapted boardwalk that has been made for him to accommodate his disabilities.

Joey, now fifteen years old, is still best mates with Kodak and in summer lazes about in the sunshine that he was deprived of for almost a decade, sometimes for so long that his keepers worry he will become dehydrated and bring him nice juicy treats.

Katie Hobbs asked us to spread the word about the plight of captive monkeys. 'The worst thing is that it's not illegal – you can't be prosecuted for keeping a monkey in these conditions as the law stands. There could be any number of monkeys living alone in garden-sheds across the country' she said 'estimated to be about 6,000 and, unless you've got ten acres of tropical rainforest in your back garden and a colony of monkeys living there, it's impossible to provide a suitable environment for them'.

After I blew a goodbye kiss to my ex-neighbour, I bought a china mug in the shop with a picture of Joey on it. I use it every morning at breakfast and think about his extraordinary life-change – for the better. In the wild capuchins live for about 15-25 years but have been known to make 45 in captivity so perhaps Joey has another happy thirty to make up for those cruel and miserable first nine in solitary confinement.

Ever since 2003, Martin and I have held annual fundraising events – first lunches and later teas, at our home to raise money for animal charities.

Each one we have held raises anything from one to two thousand pounds with different charities chosen each year. The organisation and cooking are a doddle compared to dealing with the weather. What is it going to do? It changes by the minute. Many friends brought dishes they'd cooked while others helped with the washing up and clearing up. But the unpredictable British climate meant I couldn't lay the tables till the very last minute. A sudden gust of wind or a summer shower could seriously spoil our day. Forty friends outdoors – good. Forty friends indoors - not so good. But these events have become so successful that nowadays, charities beg me to do a tea-party for them so I suppose I'll carry on until, like Ginger in the shafts of his cart, I too drop!

Our first ever lunch was in aid of the Born Free Foundation to which its founder, the lovely actress Virginia McKenna, came all the way from Surrey, joining our guests to tell them what the charity was trying to do – its mission statement being 'Keep Wildlife in the Wild'.

That same summer we had our second lunch, this time for Animals Asia, which was highlighting the plight of Moon Bears in China. To me this is about as cruel as it gets, with the bears unable to move as well as having metal catheters inserted into their gall bladders for bile extraction, suffering this painful imprisonment until they die.

Its founder, little Brit Jill Robinson, had always admired Virginia McKenna and it was Virginia who helped Jill to set up her charity. However, Jill wasn't able to join us as she lives too far away, dividing her time between Hong Kong where she lives with her dogs, and Chengdu in China where she has a sanctuary for the bears she has rescued, now having one in Vietnam, too.

Through our local shelter, The Mayhew Animal Home, which also does work abroad through its sister charity, Mayhew International, I met Marine Sgt. Pen Farthing. He brought along some of his lads and gave a slideshow at the shelter, showing pictures of his recent tour of duty in Afghanistan's Helmand Province where he had rescued over a dozen street dogs.

While the Taliban were lobbing grenades over the mud wall of their compound and they were tossing them back, Pen was feeding the stray dogs that had found their way into camp looking for food. Sniff the air, smell the Army rations! Two of the bitches Pen took in gave birth and very soon he had a dirty dozen.

In November 2006 Pen stopped a dog-fight, one of the poor dogs having just had his ears and tail cut off with scissors so his opponent would have less to hang on to. This dog was one of the many in Afghanistan being groomed for brutal dog-fights which the locals would bet on. Pen eventually rescued that dog and called him Nowzad, after the village where they found him, and brought him back to England in June 2007.

Our lunch that Sunday in late August was to raise the money to pay for Nowzad's six-month quarantine. I remembered that Pen and his then wife, Lisa, were over an hour late. When I rang his mobile to ask where the hell they were he said Lisa had set the Satnav for Hemel Hempstead instead of Hampstead! 'Why did he mess around with a Satnav?' quipped a guest, 'when he could have just parachuted in.' Why indeed!

'When I first got there and saw all the packs of wild and stray dogs I felt quite helpless' Pen told us, 'I had a job to do and didn't think I'd be able to do anything for them. But when the locals tried to organise a dog-fight in our camp I knew I had to act.

'Nowzad was never a vicious dog, he just needed food and love and food and love were precisely what he got. Nowzad came out of quarantine and was reunited with Pen on Christmas Eve that year, the money we raised paying for his six months kennelling. That Christmas two abused foreign dogs had fallen on their paws here in the UK – Nowzad, the hound from Afghanistan and Percy, our greyhound from Spain.

Soon after that lunch Pen was invalided out of the Marines, suffering with a bad back, and has since devoted himself to running his own charity Nowzad Dogs. Having adopted Nowzad while on a tour of duty, the charity's mission was to reunite other British soldiers with dogs they'd adopted in Afghanistan and is currently the only animal charity working out there, tackling the stray dog problem and giving rabies shots.

I was heartened to read in the Daily Mail in March 2014 that Wylie, the dog saved from an Afghan mob won a major prize at Crufts. Here is the story:

As a stray in Afghanistan Wylie (renamed by his new owner) was forced to fight other dogs in a ring, beaten by fans of the so-called sport and had his ears cut off. But in March 2014, Wylie happily padded into another arena entirely, at Crufts. There he was the star of the show-ring and received rapturous applause from a far friendlier crowd as he was crowned supreme champion in 'Scruffts', a contest for 'crossbreeds of mixed blood'.

The four-year-old mongrel, rescued from his ordeal in Kandahar by British soldiers, took victory lying down at the dog show, while owner Sarah Singleton fought back tears of joy. She said 'I've had him 18 months but it still chokes me to think what he's been through. He had an awful start in life and was so badly abused but to overcome it all and achieve what he has is amazing. Wylie's life would have been long over by now had it not been for Nowzad, the charity founded by former Marine Commando, Pen Farthing, that rescues dogs befriended by servicemen and aid workers in Afghanistan.

The dog was treated by the charity's Kabul clinic a number of times. Once he was rescued from being beaten by a crowd, but days later he was back after dog-fighters hacked off his ears and cut his muzzle open. Then he needed treatment for a stab wound to the chest and a severed tail, and finally thugs threw him under a car. Wylie was treated by Nowzad vets before being placed in kennels in the West Country during his quarantine. One of his regular visits was Sarah Singleton, from Yeovil, Somerset, who decided to enter him for Scruffts as a way of highlighting the work of Nowzad.

So successful were our lunches that we then had three every summer for the next six years, the number of guests sometimes reaching up to fifty. We always had someone from the charity to give a short talk telling guests how their money was being spent, and guests were given goody-bags when they left. These included the charity's leaflets to encourage them to become regular supporters.

In 2008 I had to have a hip replacement so took that summer off, starting again the following year but then doing only teas. Our cake-fests, a forerunner of 'The Great British Bake Off', are an annual get-together of friends old and new. We've been doing fundraising parties now for so long that many of our friends have become friends with one another. It's also a wonderful opportunity for us to see friends we might not otherwise have seen as well as highlighting the plight of animals the world over.

For anybody considering doing something similar, teas are much less of a hassle than lunches, starting later so I don't have to get up at six. Even better, many friends bring donations, having baked or bought cakes of every description. We've had cheese scones and fruit scones, creamy crunchy meringue Pavlovas, Victoria jam sponges, coffee and walnut cakes, chocolate fudge gateaux, chocolate and vanilla marble cakes, rich fruit-cakes, carrot-cakes, cheesecakes, lemon drizzles, plum tarts and apple pies. I've never had to bake a cake myself – yet!

One reason our fundraising events are successful is because between us Martin and I have a large database of people, so there are always enough friends to invite – essential if you want to raise a worthwhile amount of money. Then, Hampstead is a nice place to come to, it's in central London, so not out of the way, and we don't ask an inordinate amount of money, about £10 per person. We always have a speaker and ask the charity to send somebody from the top of their organization. At the same time, we try to have a celebrity, such as Virginia McKenna, Roger Mugford, TV vet Marc Abraham, actor Peter Egan or comedian Ricky Gervais, the last two being locals.

The events are not just fundraisers, they are also FUNraisers and we aim to collect at least £1,000 for each charity. Sometime it's more. We used to have raffles as well, but they became too much of a hassle so now we concentrate on the cakes, the speakers and the networking.

CHAPTER NINE

The 2010s

In 2010 we embarked on a whole new ball-game. Cruising. It was something we said we would never do, as it was only for old folks. But, hey, we were actually old folks now so it was OK. A brochure for a voyage around Indonesia and the South China Sea on a small ship, 'Discovery', made us change our minds about cruising. For me the main attraction was the island of Komodo and the chance to get close to its infamous ten foot dragons. And we weren't disappointed.

Prior to going ashore on Komodo there were a couple of safety rules - not to wear anything red, these dragons being able to see in colour and red means blood. And no menstruating women are allowed on the island, the dragons able to smell blood from as far as six miles away. Periods being a thing of the past for the women passengers, some now on Zimmer frames, this stricture only applied to the dancers and crew.

Once ashore we stepped into the Komodo National Park where we were met by our guide, armed with nothing more than a flimsy two-pronged wooden fork. In Africa guides have guns. One of the very first things he told us was that his colleague had just died from a bite by one of these creatures, unable to get to the nearest hospital in Bali in time. Too much information. We didn't need to know that.

Taking its name from the island, the Komodo dragon is a type of monitor lizard which also inhabits some of the smaller surrounding islands. They were first documented by Europeans in 1910, when they were rumoured to be 'land crocodiles'. Being the world's largest living lizard, living up to fifty years, with a tail as long as its body and growing up to ten feet and weighing up to 150 lbs., they're a very different animal from the little lizard my cousin, Fra, once brought me back from the Isle of Wight whose tail dropped off when I tried to pick it up. If I tried to pick up one of these giants by its tail, would that fall off too!

As on our walking safari, we were told to walk in single file, to keep close to one another and to the guide and to keep quiet. What if a tsetse fly stung me as one did in Zambia? Not only are these creatures carnivores but cannibals too, eating their own babies if the fancy so takes them. That's family planning taken a step too far!

We were assured that the dragons had just eaten so would be no threat to us. I still wished our guide had a gun, just in case. After walking along a dusty path through scrubby woodland for twenty minutes, we came to a clearing. There they were, silently staring at us while flicking out their yellow, deeply forked tongues. They were licking their lips, you might say, at the sight of a plump tourist, their next taste of blood.

These whoppers, the size of crocodiles and fleet of foot, bite their prey which then dies a couple of days later of infection caused by the virulent bacteria in their saliva. With a favourable breeze and its habit of swinging its head from side to side as it walks, the dragon can detect dead prey up to six miles away.

Another first for us in this Indonesian archipelago was to hear about, but not actually to taste, Kopi Luwak or Civet Coffee made from coffee berries which have been eaten by and passed through the digestive tract of the Asian Palm Civet. The civets eat the berries, but the beans inside pass through their system undigested, a unique combination of enzymes in the stomach adds to the coffee's flavour by breaking down the proteins that give coffee its bitter taste.

The beans are then defecated, washed, sun dried and lightly roasted, then becoming the most expensive coffee in the world, selling for up to £300 a kilo. Once the beans were gathered only in the wild but even the civet has now become a victim of factory farming. An American food writer on our ship actually took a taxi up to one of these farms to sample Kopi Luwak and assured us that the civets, although not free, were kept in large compounds. However, I have subsequently heard that they are now being restrained in small cages unable to move but there is some good news. Both Selfridges and Harrods have stopped selling this luxury coffee following protests by animals rights campaigners highlighting the cruel conditions in which these civet cats are kept.

Although many friends had sung the praises of Vietnam I was fearful of going there in case I came up against a dog-meat restaurant or saw cages of dogs being driven to the markets where they would be bludgeoned to death to tenderise the meat. As writer Brian Jackman once said to me on a press trip 'A carnivore should ever eat another carnivore' which I've always remembered. It is a variety of cannibalism.

However, this year we decided to brave it and although our various guides talked about eating dog, they always assured us that they didn't. As our coach drove along the highways I always kept a lookout for riders carrying dogs on their motorbikes. There are literally millions of motorbikes in Vietnam, cars being far too expensive for most people, and when you come to a red traffic light there will be a great swarm waiting for green. The locals are highly ingenious at carrying anything from plate glass windows, chairs and tables to a family of five – granny, mum and dad plus two tiny kids wedged in between them. I even saw a woman breast-feeding her baby while her husband put his foot down hard, overtaking every other bike on the road.

When we got down south we joined our riverboat 'The Amalotus' for a week of R&R, sailing up the mighty Mekong, stopping off at tiny towns and villages. One stop included the delta towns of Vinh Long and Cai Be where we visited a covered market to sample such local delicacies as snake wine. A row of bottles filled with neat alcohol were lined up on a table which contained small snakes or scorpions, inserted while still alive, drowning in it. I decided to wait for a glass of Chardonnay back on the boat. This potent brew is said to be Vietnam's answer to Viagra but I cannot vouchsafe its efficacy since none of the menfolk in our group were man enough to try it!

Our next attraction was an open market, lined with stalls on either side of a long and winding street. We stopped to watch a man steaming eggs. Son, our guide, bought one, cracked it open and there was the embryo of a baby chick which he then cut into pieces and gave to a couple of hungry kids standing there, mouths wide open – rather like the baby birds these little embryos should have become. 'It's probably the first protein they've had for a while', he told us.

From snake wine and steamed embryos it was time for the Catholic Cathedral, one of the largest I've ever seen. In front of the building, under a tree, were a pile of rusty cages. I gasped in horror as I saw a porcupine and four or five macaques incarcerated in these tiny prisons. The macaques were going stir-crazy – holding the front of their cages and rocking from side to side, performing stereotypic behaviour. I was so distressed by the plight of these poor little primates which I was told had been rescued from hunters, that I completely forgot to take a picture. However, as luck would have one of our party had taken one and emailed it to me when we got home.

Knowing Animals Asia have a Moon Bear sanctuary just north of Hanoi, I asked Jill Robinson to forward them my email for help. They duly put me in touch with a local wildlife organisation near Cai Be which rescued the macaques as well as the porcupine, releasing them into a protected area.

I would say here that if you ever see animal horrors while on holiday, don't just walk on by. Take pictures and if you can't do anything on the spot, contact an animal charity when you get home. When an Australian woman in our group heard me talking about the plight of these captive macaques she said 'It's been going on for hundreds of years and you won't be able to do anything to stop it'. As President Obama would say, 'YES YOU CAN'.

In the summer of 2010 I made two new friends in quick succession. An old friend with a lurcher was in her local pet-shop when a woman came in asking if anyone knew anything about greyhounds as she was writing a book about dogs ('Absolutely Barking' Simon & Shuster). Quick as flash our friend thought of us or, rather, Martin, being chairman of GIN. We arranged a meeting up at the Kenwood Café with this woman who turned out to be comic writer and Guardian columnist, Michele Hanson.

Three months later another friend invited us to Hampstead Town Hall for the showing of a video 'Around the World in 80 Dumps', made by a girl publicising the plight of kids living on rubbish dumps in Cambodia. In her interview afterwards, she said that her newly found charity, 'Small Steps Project', was collecting celebrity signed shoes and auctioning them to raise money to buy shoes for these poor bare-foot kids.

Not only that, but there was our Guardian columnist, Michele Hanson, and it was her daughter, Amy, who had made the video! What a wonderful coincidence. I was so impressed with what Amy was trying to do that I volunteered to help and set about collecting shoes from local celebrities.

I netted twenty pairs from the likes of Ricky Gervais and Liam Gallagher to Boy George, John le Carre and Peter Egan. It was terrific fun and, together with my haul, Amy raked in a hundred pairs, auctioned them at a party at The Royal Society for Medicine where she showed her latest video shot in Guatemala, and raised twenty grand. Not only was Peter at the party, all shoe donors being invited, but I learnt he knew Michele from having met on the Heath while walking their dogs, later doing the voice-over for Amy's next video. Strange that one of Peter's TV starring roles was in 'Ever Decreasing Circles' – the story of my life!

Fast forward to January 2014. I hadn't seen Amy since our first tea-party last summer, six months ago, although we had spoken on the phone and she'd told me that her latest shoe auction on eBay had raised FIFTY THREE THOUSAND POUNDS! Amy also decided she would like a dog so I put her in touch with Ira Moss of All Dogs

178

Matter whom I'd met five years ago up at the Kenwood café, where I have fortuitously met so many interesting people, some now friends such as Ira.

When we got back from our Christmas cruise, Ira told me that Amy had that very day got a puppy – not the French bulldog she so wanted but a dumped Staffie found tied to railings in Tower Hamlets. She was to be his foster carer to see how she got on with him. Taken to the pound, he was then rescued by one of Ira's volunteers who arranged with Amy for the handover to take place in a pet shop where they could buy him a collar and lead, arriving on the shoulders of the volunteer, the only way he could be transported. About ten months old, he had big bald patches on his dull black coat and was so thin that the skin on his huge skull made him look macabre.

Amy agreed to take Alfie on as his foster mother, and also to get him settled in before she headed off to Romania for her charity (Small Steps Project) to tackle the plight of kids living on rubbish dumps there. About a week later he had a seizure and the vet suggested she filmed the next one on her iPhone which she did. His behaviour was mostly exemplary – housetrained, obedient and affectionate, sleeping when left alone rather than tearing up Amy's flat but the seizures became more frequent and he started becoming aggressive to other dogs. When Amy tried using a training clicker on him, he went ballistic and when the vet used a scanner to check if he'd been micro-chipped, Alfie attacked him.

Ira then chanced upon something on the internet about Staffies suffering from a condition recently discovered by The Animal Health Trust, known as L2-GHA, (L2 Hydroxyglutaric Aciduria, a neurometabolic disorder found in Staffordshire Bull Terriers and appearing at about 6-10 months old), and caused by inbreeding. The condition affects the central nervous system and symptoms include epileptic seizures, stiffness, tremors, staring at walls and other altered behaviour. The severity of symptoms ranges from mild to extreme and in many cases euthanasia is necessary. Dogs can also be carriers without actually having any symptoms.'

Staffies are now bred on housing estates in large numbers but often with a small gene pool, and then sold or even given away 'TO A GOOD HOME' on the internet. This causes charities, such as ADM, big problems. Puppies are taken away from their mothers long before they are weaned and often die within days of being bought.

Every Monday, Ira gets a list from the pound of dogs with only days to go before being put down and she has to choose those she thinks she can rehome. Many are Staffies. Those she cannot, are PTS (put to sleep) – 9,000 healthy dogs a year in the UK, a so called 'Nation of Dog Lovers'. The larger ones Ira takes go to kennels in Walthamstow or Norfolk and are put up for adoption on her website. Puppies and smaller dogs, such as Yorkies, Chihuahuas, Fox-terriers and some Staffies go to foster-carers, which is where Amy came in.

But Alfie's behaviour became ever more unpredictable and bizarre, sometimes he was freaked out by such things as being offered a biscuit - by Amy. Amy was no longer able to cope with him and do her job at the same time and whether he was suffering from a brain tumour, possibly having been hit over the head, or from this condition of L2- HGA, he most certainly could not be rehomed.

Sadly, Ira (who was the official owner) and Amy decided there was no other option than to have him put down and that is what happened on 10 March, 2014, eight weeks to the day that Amy took him in. He was given an injection to sedate him and Ira sat with him stroking his head until he fell asleep when the vet gave him another injection - this time a lethal one.

This tragic story is just one of millions caused by over-breeding, resulting in dogs being dumped. Lovely girls, like my friends Ira and Amy, have to come to the rescue to try to clean up the mess made by those who treat dogs as disposable objects.

Some of the stories Ira tells me are almost unbelievable. She received a call from a single mum on an estate, with a three year old child and a three month old puppy, asking her to rehome the puppy –

not the child. A volunteer went to collect the animal and was stunned to see that its bed was in the washing machine. The puppy was so traumatised it screamed with fear when the volunteer approached and had to be taken straight to a vet to be calmed down before going to a foster carer.

The puppy, I'm glad to say, made a complete recovery but this is the kind of situation Ira meets all the time; calls from people who should never have a dog in the first place.

However, after all the heartbreakers, there are some heartwarmers, too, and fortuitously one happened shortly after Alfie's sad ending. All Dogs Matter got a call from a man who wanted a Staffie, saying he'd always had Staffies and no other breed would do. An appointment was made for him to have a look at a certain 'Smithy' who had arrived only that day from the pound in an old van. Took one look at Smithy and asked to see a few more before deciding. On hearing this Smithy picked up his lead in his mouth, jumped up on to the seat next to the man, put his paw on his shoulder and gave his cheek a lick. 'I'll take him', was the man's response. What a clever dog!

Having filled in the adoption form, said he'd get his car and made a call on his mobile. Seconds later a liveried chauffeur arrived. He placed a rug on the front seat, opened the door and in hopped Smithy. So, from arriving at the ADM office in an old van, he left in a chauffeur driven limo!

Here's a poem sent to me by a little girl, seven-year-old Hollie Pakenham Walsh.

I love dogs
I love fat dogs and thin dogs
Rescue dogs and show dogs
Skinny dogs and mini dogs
I love lazy dogs and playful dogs
Tall dogs and small dogs

I love happy dogs and sad dogs
Alert dogs and not care dogs
Fast dogs and slow dogs
I love hair dogs and bald dogs
Muddy dogs and clean dogs
Farm dogs and home dogs
But, best of all.........
Your dog loves YOU'.

I'd second that, Hollie.

The first year that I did just teas, as opposed to lunches, was 2011, when I held four tea-parties, devoting all the funds we raised to the PDSA's Pet Hospital Appeal. I held two more teas for them in 2012 and 2013, thus turning myself into a modern (geriatric?) equivalent of a Busy Bee, when I held my very first charity fundraiser in aid of the PDSA in 1940s.

In 2014, Stacey Teece of the PDSA provided me with an update of its Pet Hospital appeal:

'Our appeal was launched in 2010 with the aim of raising £6 million to fund three greatly needed PDSA Pet Hospitals, to cope with the dramatic rise in demand for our free services. Since then we have proudly opened two out of three of the facilities; a replacement Plymouth Hospital in 2012 and a replacement Cardiff hospital at the end of 2013. Our third location in Birmingham is still at the fundraising stage but we hope to begin work on this site in 2015.'

Two very exciting presents for my 80th birthday were a bronze casting of a Moon Bear for my fundraising work for Animals Asia, presented to me by Jill Robinson, and also the adoption and pictures of Oliver the bear, rescued from a crate after 30 years of having his bile extracted.

Having been a member of the British Guild of Travel Writers for 36 years, soon after my first piece was accepted by Over21, I became very upset in 2012 over the issue of foie gras. A year earlier the Canada Tourism Commission had generously hosted us at a Christmas party held in a cookery school where we cooked our own lunch. I was horrified when I saw that foie gras was included amongst the ingredients, one of the cruelest of foods. However, I seemed to be a lone voice in the wilderness when I complained, my colleagues going back for seconds. On June 13, 2013, The Sopranos actor James Gandolfini died of a heart attack in Rome – having just dined on the deadly delicacy – foie gras.

At Christmas 2012 I was pleased to see ex-007, Roger Moore, coming out against foie gras in a Christmas message in The Times, describing the cruelty involved in the production of this so-called delicacy which he so rightly calls 'torture in a tin'. And the following Christmas Sir Roger was at it again holding up a BOYCOTT FORTNUM & MASON placard together with ten animal welfare charities, including the RSPCA, Peta and the World Society for the Protection of Animals, calling for the shop to be stripped of its Royal Warrant because it continues to sell foie gras. The RSPCA says 'If you buy foie gras, you are funding the unnecessary suffering of geese and ducks'.

Sir Roger had seen undercover video footage from farms in France showing the terrible suffering endured by birds unfortunate enough to be raised for foie gras - young ducks and geese (just a few weeks old) being crammed into tiny cages barely larger than their own bodies, having two kilos of grain pumped into their crops daily. Hydraulic force-feeding machines were rolled between the cages with no escape for these imprisoned water birds and two weeks later their livers had swollen to ten times their normal size, many dying before being slaughtered. The process by which ducks and geese have their livers fattened is known as 'gavage'. For this the birds' beaks are forced open and a steel or plastic tube inserted into their mouths through which they are force-fed huge amounts of grain, enabling their livers to fatten up quickly, causing immense suffering and discomfort to the animal, and just so that this artificially- fattened liver can be enjoyed by humans.

A year later, after an AGM of the Guild held in France, which I was not permitted to attend then being only an Associate Member, I read in the monthly newsletter, 'Globetrotter', that once again members had been hosted at a cookery school and once again the main ingredient used was, yes, foie gras. I emailed those who had attended explaining how this so-called delicacy was produced, receiving either abusive replies or none at all.

I was so appalled, I resigned, my letter of resignation being published in 'Globetrotter'. As this reaches over 200 members perhaps they did me or, rather, the ducks and geese used in the production of foie gras, a favour. Here it is:

'Having been a member of the Guild for 36 years, I am now resigning. I simply cannot support an organisation in which so many members seem happy not only to consume foie gras (one of the cruelest foods) while being hosted by tourist boards but will then, presumably, write about it. Perhaps they have forgotten that for 25 years the otter (and a silver one at that) was our star award and here we are now not only tolerating but actively promoting cruelty to two species of water-fowl.

'Many EU countries have banned force-feeding while ornithologist Bill Oddie and Christine Nicol, Professor of Animal Welfare at Bristol Veterinary School, as well as many animal charities, have condemned it outright. Sir Roger Moore describes it as 'Torture in a Tin' rightly, stating that such treatment of cats and dogs would be illegal. Just click on to www.peta.org or www.ciwf.org to see what ducks and geese endure to produce this so-called delicacy. It's enough to make you want to gag!'

There was not one single letter, email or phone call of support in response, but at least I got the message across and went out with a bang! That December I read that The House of Lords was the latest institution to take foie gras off the menu. Many others, such as the

Commons, had already done so as well as restaurants and shops, from Selfridges and Harvey Nichols to Ocado and Compass (Britain's largest catering company), having now stopped serving or selling foie gras.

I read only in January 2014 that the first country to ban foie gras on grounds of animal cruelty was Nazi Germany. This is hard to believe after the cruelty they inflicted upon the Jews and other minority groups.

Yet foie gras is still sold in Fortnum Mason and served at The Ritz, The Savoy, Gordon Ramsay and The Ivy. Fortnum & Mason refuses to stop selling it, despite many demonstrations outside their Piccadilly store. But the good news is that Amazon has bowed to pressure from animal welfare campaigners to stop selling foie gras on its British website, stating 'the product, from ducks and geese that are force-fed to make their livers unnaturally large, has been added to the firm's list of prohibited items.'

VIVA!, the vegetarian and vegan campaigning charity, of which I'm a supporter, presented Amazon with video evidence of the suffering caused by producing foie gras and a petition signed by more than 10,000 opponents, of which I was just one. Production of foie gras is illegal in the UK but there is so far no ban on selling imported products.

So, if the House of Lords and Amazon have joined in the boycotting of this 'torture in a tin' why not members of The British Guild of Travel Writers, too, who have such a wonderful opportunity of spreading the word about its inhumane production? Although many retail outlets have now stopped selling foie gras, it is easily available on the internet, so there is a long way to go before this food is outlawed altogether.

At the end of 2013, Martin and I went on a wonderful Christmas cruise around the Indian Ocean on a small five-star ship. The upside was the gourmet cuisine, the downside that foie gras was served at both the Christmas and New Year's Eve gala dinners. On a tour of the kitchens, I handed the chef an anti foie gras flyer. I also gave one to the Captain as he bade us farewell, saying what a cruel delicacy it was, to which he replied 'But the passengers love it'. My response was that sometimes men love buggering little boys but that's no reason to allow them to do it.

Living in Hampstead we get used to seeing actors, writers, celebrities and wannabes of all degrees, shopping in Tesco, dining at Villa Bianca, jogging on the Heath or walking their dogs there. I've spotted Russell Brand and Ricky Gervais, Vanessa Feltz and Boy George, Derek Jacobi and John le Carre, Esther Rantzen and Peter Egan, Michael Palin, Liam Gallagher, Simon Callow and the new kid on the block, Gok Wan with his French bulldog, not forgetting Macca thirty years ago with Old English, Martha..

I'd seen local actor Peter Egan ('Ever Decreasing Circles' and dozens more notable roles) walking around the village with his dogs. Then, about five years ago Martin and I went to a PETA (People for the Ethical Treatment of Animals) fundraising lunch at a Vegan restaurant in the city. There was Peter Egan – at PETA Vegan! We chatted and he offered us a lift back to Hampstead.

A few months later I met Peter again through my friend, Ira Moss, who had just founded her own charity 'All Dogs Matter', saving dogs from Death Row, mostly dumped Staffies, now a major urban problem. Ira had met Peter on the Heath while walking their dogs (he currently has six – all rescues) and persuaded him to become Chairman of Trustees of ADM. And here were we now, toasting the opening of the charity's new offices.

We then had a fundraising tea-party for ADM in our house and Ira asked if Peter could come. Yes, please. He read a poem about a Staffie (having adopted one himself) as hundreds had been abandoned over the Christmas holiday, many being destroyed owing to lack of space in kennels. Peter cried. We cried, too.

Since that tea-party, we've met Peter regularly at Ira's annual dog show, 'Pup Idol', as well as her annual Valentine's Day and

186

Halloween Dog Walks on the Heath, so I asked him to come to the 2012 annual May Heath Walk for Animals Asia where I introduced him to AAF's PR.

Next thing I knew Peter had become their UK Ambassador, did a gig at our local venue, Burgh House, along with fellow actors Bob Daws and Amy Robbins in aid of AAF, winged his way to Chengdu for the weekend to meet Jill and see the bears in between appearing at The National Theatre in Alan Bennett's play, 'People'.

Not only that, he appeared in the 2012 Christmas Special of 'Downton Abbey' and, while shooting, got actress Leslie Nichol (Mrs. Patmore, Downton's cook), on board. Leslie and her husband then went out to Chengdu where she was filmed cooking for the bears. He also agreed to become Patron of our charity Greyhounds in Need. Not for nothing is he now known as St. Peter!

2013 was the Year of Living Dangerously for us. It started off well, Martin picking up an award on behalf of Greyhounds in Need for 'Best Rescue' at the Wetnose Animal Aid Awards in March; then Percy won 'Mr. Hampstead' at the All Dogs Matter 'Pup Idol' show in June; then the two of us were given the Animals Asia Independent Volunteer(s) Award, to be presented to us by herself, none other than darling Dr. Jill, at a Gala Evening near Henley in October organised by Peter Egan.

However, a month earlier as we were about to leave for SPANA's 90th anniversary lunch at The Kensington Roof Gardens, Martin ran upstairs to check and email and came down on his back, headfirst. I heard a great thud and a yell, ran from my dressing table to the bedroom door, to see him sliding towards me and landing at my feet.

He couldn't get up at first so I helped him to his feet, got his shoes and clothes off and into bed. We called the physio. who said to take two paracetemol and stay in bed for 24 hours and then call the doctor. We didn't hear any bones crack so presumed he'd just pulled a muscle. As I was already dressed for the lunch party, off I went. He wasn't up and running in time for Jill to present us with the award at the Gala Evening so Peter came to our house and did the honours.

Peter was also generous enough to publicly credit me with getting him involved in saving the Moon Bears at their Burgh House Christmas fund-raiser, where he performed with Bob Daws and Amy Robbins. My reply was that 'If I die tomorrow, I'll have done at least one useful thing'. I'd even go as far as to say ' the best thing I ever did'. At the end of the show a supporter donated for auction the most wonderful cake – a replica of a Moon Bear, with every whisker and claw clearly defined. When the bidding reached £200 up piped the familiar voice of our very own local celebrity, Ricky Gervais. 'I'll bid a thousand if we can cut it up and eat it after the show'. Job done. That really was having our cake and eating it!

In March 2014 the online newspaper The Huffington Post ran a story saying that a new Bill in California aims to stop the SeaWorld animal theme park from making orcas – a species of whale – from performing for the entertainment of humans. Richard Bloom, a Democratic State Assemblyman, introducing the Bill, said: 'These beautiful creatures are much too large and too intelligent to be confined in small, concrete tanks for their entire lives.' There is no justification, he added, for the continued captive display or orcas for entertainment purposes.

Calls to end the practice of keeping whales in captivity are growing and I hope it will soon be outlawed everywhere. As ever I try to put my money where my mouth is where animals are concerned, and have adopted an orca called Holly through the Whale and Dolphin Conservation Society.

Wetnose Animal Aid, another of my very favourite organisations, which raises funds to help ill-treated and abandoned animals all over the world, headed out to Romania in 2014 to film a major documentary about the illegal slaughter of street dogs, and to help those who are already out there doing their best.

The team comprised K9Angels, Norton Dog Rescue, celebrities

Lorraine Chase along with Film Director/ cameraman from SWLTV Peter Fison. The film documented the horrendous state of affairs in Romania, an EU state whose response to their street dog problem is to actively encourage their population to attack, maim, or beat to a pulp any stray animals they come across. There was also strong support from celebrities Amanda Holden and Paul O'Grady.

Many videos on YouTube show sickening scenes and atrocious acts incited by this 'final solution' mentality. What you don't always hear though are the screams of these poor innocent animals.

Not only is this incredibly cruel, counter-productive, and short sighted, but also fundamentally against the law in the EU.

The Wetnose team visited the better shelters and also the horrible places where these poor unfortunates are existing. They interviewed vets, local rescue staff, helpers and all those who could offer serious comment in a balanced and objective way, along with passion and compassion, and do their best to draw the public and the politicians attention within the EU as to the reality of what is happening.

Andrea Gamby-Boulger, who with her husband Gavin founded Wetnose in 2000 as the animal equivalent to Red Nose Day, described the situation in Romania as 'the animal equivalent to Cambodia's Killing Fields', truly nothing less.'

They had also been trying for years to have a national animal Wetnose Day on TV, like Rednose Day for kids. This year they declared Friday, 26th September to be Wetnose Day with schools , celebrities and people all over the country joining in, wearing black noses, and raising money for animal shelters. Paws crossed that 2015 Wetnose Day will be on TV!

CONCLUSION

During my seven decades in animal welfare not only have I seen, sometimes at first hand, the horrendous cruelty perpetrated upon animals, and also fish, but also observed how the animal welfare charities that I support have grown in strength and now have far more muscle than they did when I first joined them. Charities such as The Brooke, SPANA (Society for the Protection of Animals Abroad), Born Free, Animals Asia, Compassion in World Farming and International Animal Rescue have all considerably raised the profile on animal abuse both in the UK and worldwide. Their sterling work has been helped by celebrities such as Joanna Lumley and Ricky Gervais, both of whom have an enormous fan base.

Almost every charity now has a celebrity Patron and GIN (Greyhounds in Need) had an enormous stroke of luck in securing Dame Judi Dench who will now be co-Patron with fellow actor, Peter Egan as well as best-seller, Jilly Cooper.

This came about on my morning walk up to the Kenwood Cafe when a young woman jumped up to admire our handsome galgo, Percy. Martin explained to her about the plight of these designer dogs, mentioning that he was Chairman of GIN and that our very first Patron, actress and animal lover Alexandra Bastedo, had just died.

Next day we met again when she told me that she was Finty Williams, Dame Judi's daughter, and that she'd spoken to her mother (then busy filming The Best Exotic Marigold Hotel 2 in India) who had offered to replace her old friend Alex as our Patron. And that's not all. When I told her about my friend Amy Hanson's charity, Small Steps Project - raising money to put shoes on barefoot kids living on rubbish dumps - she volunteered not only to get her mother to sign a pair of her shoes but to get the whole cast from Maggie Smith, Penelope Wilton, Celia Imrie, and Bill Nighy to Tom Wilkinson and Dev Patel to do the same. That cafe should be renamed The Network Café as only days later I got a posed picture of fashionista Gok Wan with his French Bulldog, Dolly.

Although the ghastly and completely unnecessary bile trade continues in China and Vietnam, there was some truly heartening news in 2014 from Jill Robinson, founder of Animals Asia.

A new bear sanctuary – their third - is to be opened on the site of a former bile farm in Nanning, Southern China.

After many years of extracting bile from his bears and breeding them to sell, one farmer had a change of heart. He became convinced by his daughter that the bear bile trade was not only cruel, but also incompatible with his Buddhist faith. Although bile extraction ceased on the farm in 2012, lack of funds meant that the bears were uncared for, and some had been sold to a local zoo.

Animals Asia will take over the control, custody and care of the bears, building outdoor enclosures and comfortable dens and by working with the farmer and also the government, will improve the lives of more than 130 captive bears.

A question always asked is: how will those whose livelihoods depended on cruel treatment of animals make a living in the future? In this case, the new sanctuary will provide alternative jobs for the farm workers and retrain them as skilled bear carers.

The conversion of a bear farm into a sanctuary and education centre, is the largest rescue in the charity's history. To achieve this, Animals Asia has worked closely with the Chinese government and it represents a major step forward in ending the bear bile trade.

The cost of converting the site and facilities, training and paying staff and providing medical care for the bears for three years, is estimated at £3 million. Naturally, I shall do my bit by hosting fundraising events for this wonderful new sanctuary.

As to other animal matters, I would never go hunting because I would find it distressing to see any animal being set upon by hounds - be it a fox, a hare or a stag. I support The League Against Cruel Sports – 90th anniversary, 2014 but if those animals really do need to be culled, which is highly debatable, then I think it a far quicker and kinder death for foxes to be torn apart than suffering slowly by being snared, shot or poisoned which I'm told is what now happens since the Hunting Act came into force in 2006.

While the ban was being debated in Parliament, brought in by a Labour Government and taking up years of Parliamentary time, I felt it was more about 'getting toffs off horses' than genuine animal welfare. I also thought there were more pressing issues to be tackled such as the long-haul transport of food animals, ritual slaughter, factory farming and puppy farming, to name but a few. All these issues involve the suffering of thousands if not millions of animals whereas the fox does have a sporting chance of escaping. Those creatures incarcerated in crates or trucks have absolutely none!

I am, however, appalled that fur coats are coming back into fashion and that we are seeing them on the catwalk again. Fur coats are also creeping back into upmarket stores Harrods and Harvey Nichols. In fact, senior executive Paula Reed, a former fashion journalist, resigned over this issue in November 2013, unable to square the return of a fur department with her conscience.

It was also sad to see a picture of film star Catherine Deneuve aged 70, wearing a fur coat and Liz Hurley wearing what certainly looked like a fur stole at a gala Tusk event, of all places. The problem is that what celebrities do today, ordinary people will inevitably copy tomorrow.

Mark Glover of Respect for Animals (R4A) – an organisation which concentrates its efforts solely on campaigning against the international fur trade, had this to say about fur coming back on to the catwalk: 'We are disturbed by the continuing presence of fur on cat-walk shows in London during Fashion Week but they get the headlines! Despite this, the number of retail shops that are turning their backs on fur has increased. Inditex, a global clothing retailer (one of their chains is Zara) has just signed up to the first global fur free retail programme; we have a standard agreement national programme with a fur free alliance with shops and stores all over the world signing up to this such as M&S, John Lewis and Top Shop'.

Regarding leather, he said: 'R4A doesn't campaign against leather as it is a by-product of the meat trade'.

Fur farming is now banned in many countries but is a major industry in Denmark, the USA and Canada. PETA states: Before animal skins reach store shelves, animals live a life of misery, pain, boredom and fear, and many are skinned alive.

On fur farms, inquisitive and normally free-roaming animals such as foxes, minks and chinchillas spend their entire lives confined to tiny, filthy wire cages. They are denied the opportunity to engage in natural behaviours such as climbing, burrowing and swimming, and many go insane. When they are killed, animals are often gassed, anally or genitally electrocuted, or poisoned with strychnine, or their necks are snapped. These methods are not always effective: some animals actually regain consciousness while their skin is being torn off their bodies.

Needless to say, I haven't worn fur for decades but I do wear some leather.

On the subject of the Canadian seal hunt Mark says 'for the past five or six years there has been no ice in the Gulf of St. Lawrence which is terrible for the seals but at least the sealers can't get them. In 2014, because of climate change in the jet stream, the ice was so thick that the sealers' boats couldn't get out.

'The heartening news is that the EU import ban of seal products in 2010 has more or less killed the trade. The bottom has fallen out of the market and from 300,000 seals being killed every year that number dropped to 70-90,000 in 2013.'

Does he think campaigning works? 'Yes, one hundred percent. The commercial import ban on seal products which came into force in 2010 was challenged at the WTO by both Canada and Norway but the ban was upheld owing to intense campaigning. This will be seen as perhaps the single biggest step forward for animal welfare. It sets a precedent for other trading bans on an immoral trade.'

I hope that we are seeing the last gasp from the fur trade before it dies out altogether although 'Blackglama', a farmed mink company, is still in production and advertising heavily. The word 'Blackglama' comes not from 'glamour' as might be supposed, but the Great Lakes Mink Association (GLMA). Over the years film stars and celebrities such as Lauren Bacall, Naomi Campbell, Janet Jackson, Elizabeth Hurley and Elle Macpherson have been the 'face' of 'Blackglama'. Fur companies try hard to maintain their association with glamour and celebrity, hiding the cruelty by which these beautiful furs are made into expensive coats, average price, £8,000. In 2013, between 75 and 82 million mink were killed to be turned into fur coats.

Whether fur animals are farmed or trapped makes no difference to the cruelty. On fur farms, mink, for instance, are kept in tiny cages crammed together, while in the wild they are solitary, semi-aquatic creatures which only come together for reproduction purposes. If trapped by the brutal leghold method, fur animals can be in agony for days, often trying to chew off their own legs to escape. There is no justification whatever for the continued use of animal fur as human clothing, and it is a great shame that in some quarters anti-fur campaigns are seen as a yesterday's issue and old-fashioned. It is also sad to see that some models who once appeared in these campaigns are now themselves wearing fur down the catwalk.

This is one reason I admire Stella McCartney. A highly successful fashion designer, she has pledged never to use fur, animal skins or leather; a promise she has kept. Her website states:

'We do not use leather, skins or furs in any of our products or licensed products. We also make sure that none of our glues contain animal products'.

McCartney admits that using synthetic or woven materials is more difficult for shoes than leather and as a result, all her shoes and bags are made by hand; often costing 70% more to make than a leather equivalent.

A question I am often asked, given my views on fur, is: is it OK to wear false fur – or faux as it's usually known these days? Obviously it's better to wear faux fur than the real thing but it's often difficult to tell the difference and that is what the fur trade wants. Nowadays, I wouldn't even wear faux. It's cheaper to breed dogs in China and then dye their fur, using it for trimming on anoraks and coats, than to make faux fur. I have often been into shops, felt the 'fur', know that is it real, and then the assistant tells me it's fake.

Either she is dumb or has been told to say it's fake by her boss, in case the customer is an anti-fur activist.

On the difficult and controversial issue of scientific and medical testing on animals, I am a strong supporter of BUAV, which uncompromisingly campaigns against ALL such experiments. Chief executive Michelle Thew says: 'Our principal objection is moral, opposing the suffering to animals that such experiments represent.'

Increasingly, she says, there is evidence which demonstrates that testing on animals is not productive, especially when it comes to developing drugs for human use. She adds: ' Animals do not get many of the diseases that humans do, such as heart disease, many types of cancer, HIV, Parkinson's disease or schizophrenia. These have to be artificially induced in the animal and the resulting 'animal models' are usually crude and incomplete representations of the human disease.' Michelle goes even further and declares that there is very little scientific evidence for claims that animal tests have saved human lives.

Another point made by the BUAV is that if humans took more care of themselves, there would be far less need for many of today's drugs, most of which are tested on animals.

Of course, there is also a powerful pro-animal testing lobby and the controversy continues. But in common with most other animal welfare groups, BUAV believes that constant campaigning is their most effective – possibly their only effective – tool. Among their successes is the launch in 2012 of Cruelty Free International, a global organization dedicated to ending product testing on animals worldwide. India and Israel have followed the EU on cosmetics testing on animals. All Sainsbury's own brand cosmetics now carry the Leaping Bunny cruelty-free logo.

Also in 2012, a vigorous campaign stopped a planning application to breed and supply beagles to laboratories for experimentation. Some older readers may remember the Sunday People investigation in the 1970s, where reporter Mary Beith went undercover in a research station and secretly photographed hundreds of beagles in cages, being forced to smoke cigarettes. The nation was appalled, and later this story was followed up by Shan Davies's investigation, again for the Sunday People, into a farm where beagles were bred specifically for laboratory research.

These stories appeared more than 30 years ago, and still the cruelty continues, prevented only when organisations such as the BUAV campaign against it.

Again owing to intense campaigning, American Airlines, Caribbean Airlines and Monarch Air have stopped transporting monkeys destined for research.

As to wildlife, Charlie Mayhew, founder and CEO of Tusk Trust in 1990 along with actor Timothy Ackroyd, and supported by Prince William, does not mince his words:

'The Illegal Wildlife trade is a real stain on our global society, responsible for the decimation of many species, not least of all elephant, rhino and lion. Tusk has been working closely with the British Government throughout 2013 to help garner real international collaboration and momentum to halt the sickening trade in products such as ivory and rhino horn.

'With the significant support of our patron Prince William and his father the Prince of Wales, we have recently seen some significant steps taken by the international community at the London Conference to clamp down on the trade. There is a real sense of momentum and at last we appear to have political will to tackle the issue. The fact that the profits from this illegal trade are being mercilessly exploited by sophisticated criminal gangs and terrorist groups to underpin their operations has undoubtedly pushed the issue much further up the political agenda.

'There is finally a real sense of collaboration amongst the conservation and political community, which is heartening, and we are seeing some encouraging movements within the consumer nations that gives me hope that all is not lost. I cannot accept that we could be the generation that allowed some of Africa's most iconic species to disappear from this planet. We need a combination of demand reduction and consumer awareness programmes in the Far East as well as greater law enforcement and judicial penalties across the world to eradicate this appalling trade.'

Apart from those matters mentioned above, my own priorities for urgent action are:

Stopping longhaul transport of live food animals whether by truck or by ship; they should be on the hook not on the hoof.

Outlawing ALL testing of cosmetics on animals.

Banning ritual slaughter. It's ridiculous that any group of people should be exempt from a ban already in place prohibiting animals being slaughtered without prior stunning.

Taking action against horses in the UK being dumped on grass verges with some 7,000 currently at risk.

Campaigning for the compulsory neutering of all cats and dogs to cut down on the number of healthy animals being destroyed as being 'surplus to requirements'.

Banning bullfighting.

Banning fur farming.

Banning the production of foie gras.

Banning bear bile farming in China and Viet Nam.

Banning puppy farming in the UK.

Halting the spread of factory farming which is not only a health hazard for animals but for people, too.

Highlighting the plight of orangutans due to the loss of their habitat because of palm oil plantations.

Highlighting the plight of greyhounds – those used for racing as well as for hunting.

Banning the primate pet trade worldwide (still legal in the UK)

Last but not least, stopping the horrendous poaching of elephant and rhino for their tusks and horn – before it's too late and these two magnificent species are lost forever. The lion is also now at risk with a mere 20,000 left in the wild.

These are, to my mind, some of the most pressing animal welfare issues that should now concern us all, and that the welfare of all animals becomes uppermost in people's minds, and put before considerations of what humans might enjoy.

Compassion in World Farming has this to say about the most urgent concerns today regarding food and farm animals:

'While we do not want to get into religious arguments, we believe that the welfare of the animal must always come first, and this is why we campaign for humane slaughter without suffering.

'We value religious freedom but do not believe this should extend to any practice which inflicts suffering on animals and we will continue to campaign for the removal of exemptions from UK and EU legislation.

'We also campaign for better enforcement and regulation around slaughter in general, and would like to see the introduction of CCTV in all slaughter houses.

'With regard to live exports of sheep and other animals from Australia, which is a huge business, we are aware that millions of animals suffer hugely during these long voyages. They face brutal and violent handling, slaughter without pre-stunning and dying slow, painful deaths at the hands of untrained slaughtermen. We are campaigning, along with Animals Australia, for an end to this terrible trade.'

The mega-dairies issue, now becoming urgent in the UK as big business puts in planning applications for 8000+ cow farms, arguing that these dairies provide cheap meat, milk and also and jobs, is at the forefront of CIWF's campaigning.

Dil Peeling, CIWF director of campaigns, says:

'The rise of mega dairies has come about largely because of continual erosion of prices in the dairy industry. Many farmers are going out of business and view mega dairies as a way of bringing profits back. Large-scale businesses are in a better position than one-man operations to step into this market and many are simply not bothered about animal welfare.'

The dairy industry, adds Dil, is a complex one with no easy answers but the most important thing is that producers receive a fair price for their products. While the cost of milk and other dairy products keeps being driven down, the threat of mega-dairies, where cows will never see the light of day or graze on grass, remains.

'At the moment, the current livestock production model inflicts damage on global food security, human health and livelihoods and of course, on the animals used in the system. We desperately need to develop a food and farming system that respects animal sentience and we see this as the biggest problem facing us right now.'

So – there is still a long way to go and absolutely no room for complacency. I am so glad that younger people are now taking up the cudgels and campaigning ever harder for animals to be treated with the respect they deserve. The more you think about it, the more indefensible it becomes to abuse animals in any way. As the PETA manifesto states, 'Animals are not ours to do as we like with'.

One might imagine that animals bred as pets would be better treated. But no. TV vet Marc Abraham, founder of the British organization, PupAid, states uncompromisingly: 'Puppy farming is cruel'. He goes on: 'The commercial mass production of puppies in horrific conditions often with no clean water, quality food, medicine, even waste clearance, goes on day-in, day-out all over our 'nation of animal lovers'.

'Tragically it's commonplace for over 200 breeding bitches and stud dogs to be imprisoned – 'farmed' - in one of hundreds of large concrete agricultural sheds (typically in rural SW Wales), sadly just kept alive for the sole purpose of making puppies for profit.

'Separated from their mums too early, these puppies are then transported long distances and sold by third parties (including pet shops, websites, garden centres, puppy supermarkets, dealers, free newspaper adverts/listings); basically anywhere miles away from the pup's mum and birthplace. Unsurprisingly puppy farmed dogs are severely inbred, suffering serious internal problems (e.g. heart, eyes, joints), infectious diseases (e.g. deadly parvovirus), as well as behavioural issues (e.g. nervous aggression); meaning if they survive their first week in their new home they'll suffer a future of ill health and pain costing hundreds (sometimes thousands) of pounds to treat.

'So why is puppy farming allowed? Well once the authorities – who are meant to guard our nation's animal welfare needs - ignore a perfectly equipped Animal Welfare Act - it's then mostly legal with both Breeding and Pet Shop licences handed out like candy to greedy kids.

So how do we stop this level of animal cruelty if existing legislation isn't being enforced?

'Only by stopping the demand of pups bred in this way would sales slow down, eventually helping to end production and making these battery farms for dogs both unprofitable and useless.

'PupAid's campaign raises awareness to stop demand for poorly pups by educating the public in the correct way to choose a dog, i.e. from the thousands stuck in rescue or ask "Where's Mum?" and insisting on seeing her interacting with her pups.

'Our annual celebrity-judged fun dog show, plus the highly successful government e-petition (launched in 2013) with over 110,000 signatures (making it the biggest pet welfare e-petition of all time) calls for a ban of the sale of puppies without their mums, and thus ending the supply/demand pipeline to the consumer.

Just one last coincidence. I discovered from Marc Abraham's mother that she and Dame Judi Dench gave birth on the very same day at the very same hospital in adjoining rooms to their babies, Marc and Finty. Ever decreasing circles!

In my more than seven decades devoted to animal welfare, I take heart from the many wonderful, kind and caring people I've met who are doing everything they can to alleviate animal suffering from fundraising and campaigning to setting up sanctuaries and working in the field as vets.

Alan Knight, CEO of International Animal Rescue, once said to me 'We don't want to get bigger, we want to go out of business - not through lack of funds but because there is no longer any need for our services.'

We cannot have two hearts, one for the animals, the other for man. In cruelty toward the former and cruelty toward the latter there is no difference but in the victim'(Alphonse Marie Louis de Lamartine, 1790-1869).

And now for the good news. And good news there is aplenty! 2014 was the year that Joey's erstwhile owner, got her comeuppance! The story of THE BAD SAMARITAN had lain dormant, as far as I knew, since that piece by Tim Rayment appeared in The Sunday Times Magazine in November 2008. However, on Thursday, 1st May this year both our local newspapers ran a story about a middle-aged blonde, Juliette d'Souza, on trial for fraud. At first, not particularly interested, I read on and what caught my eye was that she had once owned a monkey! Yes, it was our ex-neighbour, Vanessa Campbell, Joey's owner.

Next day I hot-footed it down to Blackfriars Crown Court to see for myself, at close quarters, this extraordinary woman who had ruined so any people's lives, as well as that of her pet monkey, Joey.

As luck would have it, Tim Rayment, was in the Witness Box that very day. He was cross-questioned about his Sunday Times Magazine story but no-one (neither the Prosecution nor the Defence Counsels and not even Rayment himself) actually had a copy. It had been downloaded from the Internet but there were no pictures. Her Defence Counsel claimed that Rayment had never been to Surinam where he said he had tried to interview her. There was a picture of her taken there getting into her car which had local number plates, taken by Rayment's photographer. Luckily, I had brought with me my 'JOEY FILE' of all the newspaper cuttings about my adopted monkey.

Being in the front row of the Public Gallery, I held it open at the relevant page for Rayment to see. He nearly fell out of the Witness Box with surprise. Turning to the Judge he said 'My Lord, there is a copy in this courtroom being held by someone in the Public Gallery.' Instead of being thrown out of Court, the Judge asked me to hold it up for all to see. At lunchtime, a Detective Inspector on the case, approached me and asked 'How are you implicated with this woman?' I replied that I had only ever seen her a couple of times in our street but that I'd adopted her monkey!' He then asked if he could borrow the Sunday Times Magazine to photocopy the story for evidence.

The following day she was found guilty on all 23 charges of fraud and given ten years in the slammer. JUSTICE FOR JOEY at last! We made plans to visit him early in September, when our fundraising parties were over, to celebrate the end of this extraordinary saga.

But first the fundraisers. We missed a Gala Dinner in aid of Animals Asia held at 'Gilgamesh' in Camden Town at which half a dozen of the 'Downton Abbey' cast were performing because we were on a river-cruise from Amsterdam to Budapest. However, Jill Robinson would still be in London when we got back so we slotted in an extra party a 'bubbly and bites', raising the 2014 summer series to FIVE, and had a bumper turnout of fifty five with John Rendall, owner of Christian the lion as well as local heroes actor Peter Egan and comedian Ricky Gervias. Jill had cleverly discovered that it was Ricky's birthday and she presented him with a picture of a bear named 'Derek' after his current TV series. Then we all sang HAPPY BIRTHDAY to him.

The next four parties were teas – kicking off with SPANA (Society for the Protection of Animals Abroad), then All dogs Matter, then Nowzad Dogs, with Pen Farthing actually arriving on time. This was a sad day for Pen, though, because seven years earlier when we'd had our first lunch to raise funds for his dog Nowzad's quarantine, here we were all these years later commiserating with Pen who had to have Nowzad put down only the previous day. It seemed we'd come full circle with that dog – first celebrating his rescue and arrival in the UK and now his early demise. As the weather was so uncertain I lay awake all night before all of the parties, wondering if we were going to be rained on, and so after our last one for Compassion in World Farming, at which we all held up acopy of 'Farmageddon' which made the Ham & High, we decided to call it a day and quite while still winning!

John Rendall sent us an invitation to the George Adamson Wildlife Preservation Trust's 25th Anniversary to be held on 25th September at The Royal Geographical Society of which I'm a Fellow. The very first person clapped eyes on was John's friend, photographer of all those Christian the Lion pictures, Derek Cattani. Camera slung around his neck, I asked if he was here working. 'No', he said, 'but if I ever leave my camera at home, something exciting happens!' 'Any celebs. here?' I wondered. 'Only the actress who played 'M' in the last Bond movie' he replied 'but I can't remember her name'. 'Judi Dench?' 'That's her!' he laughed. I nearly fainted with excitement, as she was now our very newest Patron of 'Greyhounds in Need'.

Looking around for a sighting of Dame Judi, I discovered her sitting with two friends in the front row of the empty adjoining room, set up for the film-show and talk to be given by none other than Tony Fitzjohn. I grabbed Martin by the elbow and said 'go for it - introduce yourself to Dame Judi'. He did so with great aplomb and she was most enthusiastic at being GIN's new patron. Even better, I also grabbed Derek Cattani and said that if he could get a picture of Martin with Dame Judi, I would donate £100 to GAWPT. Dame Judi graciously posed after the lecture and the picture appears here in this book and the cheque is not just 'in the post' but actually in GAWPT's bank account. Job done!

And, finally, Percy, once so scared we couldn't even look him in the eye, and so petrified by all the people at his first garden party that he had to be restrained with two leads otherwise he'd have done a runner has, over the past seven years, become a relaxed and affectionate dog, galloping out into the garden at our summer parties to greet our guests.

I can truly say that he, too, is now a party animal!

PS. The very day that I finished this book (dedicated to Percy the 'galgo', Joey the Capuchin Monkey and Oliver the Moon Bear), I got an email from Jill Robinson in Chengdu, China, 'so very sorry,

Angela – we said goodbye to your boy this afternoon and it seemed the whole world cried....well, at least in our world. He'll be so missed and will be buried tomorrow morning. Bear hugs, Jill'. After 30 years of Bear Hell, Oliver did have 4 years of Bear Heaven – a happy ending.

APPENDIX

These are the animal charities we have held fundraising lunches and teas for, attended by celebrities from Virginia McKenna, actor Peter Egan, animal behaviourist Dr. Roger Mugford, TV Vet Marc Abraham, and last, but not least, comedian, actor, writer and director and local Hampstead resident, Ricky Gervais.

Animals Asia, Born Free, Compassion in World Farming, PDSA, The Brooke, SPANA, The Mayhew Animal Home, Wood Green, International Animal Welfare, Nowzad Dogs, Greek Animal Welfare Fund, World Society for the Protection of Animals, Home and Abroad Animal Welfare, Environmental Investigation Agency, All Dogs Matter and, of course, Greyhounds in Need, some of which I've done twice or more.

In over a decade we've covered organisations addressing such abuses as bear bile farming and the dog meat trade in China and Viet Nam; zoos and circuses around the world; wildlife poaching in Africa; long haul transport and factory farming of food animals; the dancing bear trade in India and the plight of orangutans in Borneo. We've also raised funds for the rescue and rehoming of abandoned or cruelly treated dogs in Afghanistan, Spain, Sri Lanka and here in the UK as well as protecting turtle eggs in the Greek Islands, and giving free vet treatment to working horses, mules and donkeys in the developing world.

CONTACTS FOR ANIMAL CHARITIES/ORGANISATIONS

All Dogs Matter,
30, Aylmer Parade,
Aylmer Road,
London N2 0PH

Tel: 020-8341-3196
Email: info@alldogsmatter.co.uk
www.alldogsmatter.co.uk

All Dogs Matter rescues and rehomes abandoned dogs that are on Death Row in London pounds.

Anglo-Italian Society for the Protection of Animals,
30-34, New Bridge Street,
London, EC4V 6BJ.

Tel/Fax: 01743-232559
Email: info@aispa.org.uk
Website: www.aispa.org.uk

AISPA is a British-based charity that raises funds worldwide to help animal welfare projects in Italy.

Animal Aid,
The Old Chapel,
Bradford Street,
Tonbridge, Kent TN9 1AW

Tel: 01732-364546
Email: info@animalaid.org.uk

Website: www.animalaid.org.uk

Hard hitting campaigns to put pressure on charity-funded vivisection; fighting the Grand National death trap and promoting a meat free lifestyle.

Animals Asia Foundation,
3, Ashleigh Meadow,
Tregondale Farm,
Menheniot, Cornwall, PL14 3RG.

Tel: 01579-347-148
Email: info@animalsasia.org
Website: www.animalsasia.org

Animals Asia is dedicated to ending the barbaric practice of bear bile farming and improving the welfare of animals in China and Vietnam.

Animal Defenders International (ADI),
Millbank Tower, Millbank,
London SW1P 4QP.

Tel: 020-7630-3340
Fax:020-7828-2179
Website: www.ad-international.org

Campaigns against animal abuse worldwide from animal experimentation to circuses and zoos.
Animal Health Trust,
Lanwades Park, Kentford,
Newmarket,Suffolk CB8 7UU&.

Tel: 01638-555648
Email: info@aht.org.uk
Website: www.aht.org.uk

Carrying out research into animal diseases such as L-2 HGA
from which Staffordshire Bull Terriers sometimes suffer.

The Bat Conservation Trust,
15, Cloisters House,
8, Battersea Park road,
London SW8 4BG.

Tel: 0845-1300-228
Email. enquiries@bats.org.uk
Website: www.bats.org.uk

Protecting bats and their habitat.

The Blue Cross,
Shilton Road, Burford,
Oxon OX18 4PF.

Tel: 0300-777-1897
Email: info@bluecross.org.uk
Website: www.bluecross.org.uk

Helping sick, injured and homeless pets from dogs and cats to
horses.

Born Free Foundation,
3, Grove House,
Foundry Lane,
Horsham, RH13 5PL

Tel: 01403-240170
Email: info@bornfree.org.uk
Website: www.bornfree.org.uk

Born Free is an international wildlife charity working throughout the world to protect individual wild animals from suffering and to protect threatened species in the wild.

Bransby Horses,
Bransby, Lincoln LN1 2PH.

Tel: 01427-788464
Email: mail@bransbyhorses.co.uk
Website: www.bransbyhorses.co.uk

Rescue and welfare of horses.

The Brooke,
5th Floor, Friars Bridge Court,
41-45, Blackfriars Road,
London SE1 8NZ.

Tel: 020-3012-3456
Email: info@thebrooke.org
Website: www.thebrooke.org
An international animal welfare organisation dedicated to improving the lives of working horses, donkeys and mules, through veterinary treatment and community programmes, in the world's poorest countries.

Butterfly Conservation,
Manor Yard, East Lulworth,
Wareham, Dorset BH20 5QP.

Tel: 01929-400209
Email: info@butterfly-conservation.org
Website: www.butterfly-conservation.org

Saving butterflies, moths and our environment.

Campaign to Protect Rural England (CPRE),
5-11,Lavington Street,
London SE1 ONZ.

Tel: 020-7981-2800
Email: info@cpre.org.uk
Website: www.cpre.org.uk

Does what it says on the tin! Campaigns to protect rural England.

Captive Animals Protection Society (CAPS),
P.0. Box 540,
Salford M5 ODS.

Tel: 0845-330-3911
Email: info@captiveanimals.org
Website: www.captiveanimals.org

Working since 1957 for a world without cages.

Care for the Wild International,
72, Brighton Road, Horsham,
West Sussex RH13 5BU.

Tel: 01403-249832
Email: info@careforthewild.com

Website: www.careforthewild.com

For the past 30 years has been campaigning to protect wildlife and educating the next generation to care for the wild.

Cats Protection,
National Cat Centre,
Chelwood Gate,
Sussex RH17 7TT.

Tel: 08707-708-649
Email: see website
Website: www.cats.org

Rescues and rehomes cats and campaigns for neutering.

Celia Hammond Animal Trust (CHAT),
High Street, Wadhurst,
East Sussex TN5 6AG.

Tel: 01892-783367
Email: headoffice@celiahammond.org
Website: www.celiahammond.org

Celia Hammond rescues and rehomes cats, and promotes neutering.

Compassion in World Farming,
River Court, Mill Lane,
Godalming, Surrey, GU7 1EZ.
Tel: 01483-521-950
Email: compassion@ciwf.org
Website: www.ciwf.org

CIWF is the leading international farm animal welfare charity, bringing about bans on veal crates, cages for hens and sow stalls and campaigns against long-haul transport of food animals.

The David Sheldrick Wildlife Trust,
2nd Floor, 3 Bridge Street,
Leatherhead, KT22 8BL.

Tel: 01372-378-321
Email: infouk@sheldrickwildlifetrust.org
Website: www.sheldrickwildlifetrust.org

Embracing measures for the protection of wildlife and conservation of wild habitats in Kenya; also runs the famous elephant orphanage outside Nairobi. A must see!

Dogs Trust,
17, Wakley Street,
London EC1V 7RQ.

Tel: 202-7837-0006
Email: see website
Website: www.dogstrust.org.uk

With 19 rehoming centres, Dogs Trust were able to look after some 17,000 dogs last year. No healthy dog ever put down.

The Donkey Sanctuary,
Slade House Farm,
Sidmouth,
Devon EX10 0NU.
Tel:01395-578222
Email: enquiries@thedonkeysanctuary.org.uk

Website: www.thedonkeysanctuary.org.uk

The Donkey Sanctuary rescues sick, injured and abandoned donkeys both here abroad.

eia (environmental investigation agency),
62-63 Upper Street,
London N1 ONY.

Tel: 020-7354-7960
Email: ukinfo@eia-international.org
Website: www.eia-international.org

Investigating the illegal trade in logging and wildlife.

Friends of the Earth,
The Printworks, 1st Floor,
139, Clapham Road,
London SW9 0HP.

Tel: 020-7490-15545
Email: see website
Website: www.foe.org.uk

An environmental organisation protecting the planet and saving bees – vital pollinators.

The Gorilla Organisation,
110, Gloucester Avenue,
London NW1 8HX.

Tel: 020-7916-4974
Email: info@gorillas.org

Website: www.gorillas.org

Provides funding for rangers to protect gorillas in the wild.

Greek Animal Welfare Fund,
51, Borough High Street,
London, SE1 1NB.

Tel: 020-7357-8500
Email: gawf@gawf.org.uk
Website: www.animalactiongreece.gr

GAWF operates in Greece as Animal Action, striving to improve the welfare of all animals in Greece.

Greyhounds in Need,
33, High Street,
Wraysbury,
Middx. TW19 5DA

Tel: 01784-483206
Email: info@greyhoundsinneed.co.uk
Website: www.greyhoundsinneed.co.uk

Dedicated to the welfare, rescue and rehoming of greyhounds, especially those in Spain.

Home & Abroad Animal Welfare,
39, Albert Street, Fleet,
Hants. GU13 9RL and
128, Buxhall Crescent,
London E9 5JZ.

Tel: 01252-629-044/079299-69148
Email: info@homeandabroadanimalwelfare.org
Website: www.homeandabroadanimalwelfare.org

Works specifically in Sri Lanka rescuing, rehoming and providing neutering and veterinary treatment for stray animals.

The Horse Trust, (Home of Rest for Horses),
Speen, Princes Risborough,
Bucks. HP27 OPP.

Tel: 0149-488464
Email: info@horsetrust.org.uk
Website: www.horsetrust.org.uk

Working to save horses from abuse and neglect.

International Animal Rescue,
Lime House, Regency Close,
Uckfield, East Sussex, TN22 1DS.

Tel: 01825—767-688
Email: info@internationalanimalrescue.org
Website: www.internationalanimalrescue.org

IAR is dedicated to the rescue and rehabilitation of suffering animals around the world, whenever possible returning animals to their natural environment but providing a permanent sanctuary for those unable to fend for themselves.

Japan Animal Welfare Fund UK, (JAWS),
Lyell House, 51 Greencoat Place,
London SW1P 1DS.

Tel: 020-7630-5563
Email: jawsuk@jawsuk.org.uk
Website: www.jawsuk.org.uk

JAWS exists to combat animal cruelty and neglect, mostly in Japan. Also to instil greater awareness and compassion for animals and to provide funding for the training of animal welfare inspectors in Japan.

The Mayhew Animal Home & Humane Education Centre,
Trenmar Gardens, Kensal Green,
London NW10 6BJ.

Tel: 020-8969-8009
Email: info@mayhewanimalhome.org
Website: www.mayhewanimalhome.org

Helping animals in need gain a better quality of life by delivering a broad range of community based animal care, education and welfare projects. Rehomes unwanted pets.

Nowzad Dogs,
P.0. Box 39,
Plymouth PL2 9AU.

Tel: 07583-812-091
Email: pen@nowzad.com
Website: www.nowzad.com

Rescuing stray and abandoned animals in Afghanistan.
Run by a staff of just two so response to emails and telephone calls may not be immediate!

The Owl Sanctuary,
16, Foxfield Road,
Barrow-in-Furness,
Cumbria, LA14 3SJ.

Website: www.wingsoverwalney.co.uk

A new, small UK based charity committed to the rescue,
rehabilitation/conservation of owls and wild birds of prey.

PETA (People for the Ethical Treatment of Animals),
Society Building,
8, All Saints Street,
London N1 9RL.

Tel: 020-7837-6327
Email: info@peta.org.uk
Website: www.PETA.org.uk

Hard hitting campaigns against the production of 'foie gras' and
other animal abuse worldwide.

PDSA,
Whitechapel Way,
Priorslee, Telford,
Shropshire TF2 9PQ.
Tel: 0800-917-2509/01952-290999
Fax: 0845-556-4906:
Website: www.pdsa.org.uk

For pets in need of vets.

Peoples Trust for Endangered Species,

15, Cloisters House,
8, Battersea Park Road,
London SW8 4BG.

Tel: 020-7498-4533
Email: enquiries@ptes.org
Website: www.ptes.org

Protecting our endangered species with a current campaign to save the hedgehog.

PupAid

Email: info@pupaid.org
Website: www.pupaid.org
Twitter @pupaid, FB Pup Aid

Campaigns against puppy farming

Redwings Horse Sanctuary,
Hapton,
Norwich, NR15 1SP.

Tel: 01508-481000
Email: info@redwings.co.uk
Website: www.redwings.org.uk

With over 6,000 horses currently at risk the charity's purpose is to provide and promote the welfare, care and protection of horses, ponies, donkeys and mules.

respect for animals,
P.0. Box 6500,

Nottingham, NG4 3BG.

Fighting the international fur trade

Royal Society for the Prevention of Cruelty to Animals (RSPCA),
Wilberforce Way,
Southwater, Horsham,
West Sussex RH13 9RS,

Tel: 0300-123-0100
Email: see website
Website: www.rspca.org.uk

Royal Society for the Protection of Birds (RSPB),
The Lodge, Sandy,
Beds. SG19 2DL

Tel: 01767-680-551
Email: see website
Website: www.rspb.org.uk

Speaks out for birds and wildlife, tackling problems which
threaten our environment.

Save the Rhino International,
16, Winchester Walk,
London SE1 9AQ.

Tel: 020-7357-7474
Fax: 020-7357-9666
Email: info@savetherhino.org
Website: www.savetherhino.org

Campaigning to save the rhino from extinction. With the current rhino poaching crisis they are funding more rangers and ensuring that local communities benefit from conservation activities.

Small Steps Project,
1b, Waterlow Road
London N19 5NJ.

Tel: 020-7272-3363
Email: info@smallstepsproject.org
Website: www.smallstepsproject.org

Small Steps Project is a humanitarian organisation and UK charity supporting children and their families living on rubbish dumps.

Soi Dog Foundation. A Phuket based charity. Rescues and cares for thousands of dogs in Thailand. Also works to end cat/dog meat trade throughout the region. To see video click on https://savedogs.soidog.org/petition

Soi Dog UK,
12, Rowan Lane,
Hellifield,
N. Yorks. BD23 4JG.

Soil Association,
South Plaza, Marlborough Street,
Bristol BS1 3NX.

Tel: 0117-314-5000
Fax: 0117-314-5001

Website: www.soilassociation.org

Campaigns for planet-friendly food and farming.

SPANA (Society for the Protection of Animals Abroad),
14, John Street,
London WC1N 2EB.

Tel:020-7831-3999
Email: info@spana.org
Website: www.spana.org

SPANA provides veterinary care to working animals - hundreds
of thousands of horses, donkeys, mules and camels - across the
developing world each year and promotes animal welfare through
education and training.

Soil Association,
South Plaza, Marlborough Street,
Bristol BS1 3NX.

Tel: 0117-314-5000
Fax: 0117-314-5001
Website: www.soilassociation.org
An environmental organisation caring for our soil, promoting
organic farming as opposed to factory farming and saving the
endangered bumblebee – our great pollinator.

The Swan Sanctuary,
Felix Lane, Shepperton,
Middx. TW17 8NN.

Tel: 01932-240-790

Email: Use telephone – maybe too busy to check emails
Website: www.theswansanctuary.org.uk

A wildlife hospital dedicated to the treatment, care and
rehabilitation of swans and wildfowl in the UK.
Tusk Trust,
4,Cheapside House,
High Street,
Gillingham, Dorset SP8 4

Tel: 01747-831-005
Email: info@tusk.org
Website: www.tusk.org

Protecting wildlife for the past 20 years in Africa. Currently
supports 57 field projects in 18 African countries and promotes
education.

Viva!
8, York Court, Wilder Street,
Bristol BS2 8QH.

Tel: 0117-944-1000
Email: info@viva.org.uk
Website: www.viva.org.uk

Animal welfare organisation campaigning against abuse and
promoting a meat free lifestyle. One billion animals are
slaughtered every year in the UK alone.

Wetnose Animal Aid,
Newgate Lodge,
7, Newgate, Kirby Cane,

Bungay, Suffolk.

Tel: 01508-518650
Email: andrea@wetnoseanimalaid.com
Website: www.wetnoseanimalaid.com

Wetnose Animal Aid fundraises to help sick and needy animals globally.

Whale and Dolphin Conservation (WDC),
Brookfield House,
38, St. Paul Street,
Chippenham,
Wiltshire, SN15 1LJ.

Tel: 01249-449-500
Email: info@whales.org
Website: www.whales.org

'A world where every whale and dolphin is safe and free'.

Wild Futures (formerly known as The Monkey Sanctuary),
Murrayton House, St. Martins,
Looe, Cornwall, PL13 1NZ.

Tel: 0844-272-1271
Email: info@wildfutures.org
Website: www.wildfutures.org

Wild Futures protects primates and habitats worldwide, and also rescues and rehabilitates those from the pet trade.

Wood Green, The Animals Charity,

Kings Bush Farm, London Road,
Godmanchester, Cambs. PE29 2NH.

Tel: 0844-248-8181
Email: see website
Website: www.woodgreen.org.uk

Wood Green rehomes not only cats and dogs but many chickens,
rabbits, mice, guinea-pigs, goats, sheep, ferrets and more! Also
provides support, guidance and education to both new and
existing pet owners.

World Horse Welfare,
Anne Colvin House,
Snetterton,
Norfolk, NR 16 2LR.

Tel: 01953-498-682
Email: info@worldhorsewelfare.org
Website: www.worldhorsewelfare.org

World Horse Welfare is a leading international charity working
to improve the lives of horses in the UK and around the world
through education, campaigns and hands-on work with horses.

World Land Trust,
Blyth House,
Bridge Street,
Halesworth, Suffolk 1P 8AB

Tel: 01986-874422
Email: info@worldlandtrust.org
Website: www.worldlandtrust.org

Buys up acres of land to save rainforests and protect endangered wildlife.

World Wildlife Fund-UK,
The Living Planet Centre,
Rufford House,
Brewery Road,
Woking, Surrey GU21 4LL.

Tel: 01483-426333
Email: supportercare@wwf.org.uk
Website: www.wwf.org.uk

Safeguarding the natural world.

WSPA (World Society for the Protection of Animals),
222, Grays Inn Road,
London WC1X 8HB.

Tel: 020-7239-0500
Email: wspa@wspa.org.uk
Website: www.wspa.org.uk

An umbrella organisation of animal welfare charities worldwide.

ACKNOWLEDGEMENTS

Thanks to Liz Hodgkinson for suggesting that I write this book- about the animal stories in my life.

Thanks to my nephew, Rupert Vandervell, for donating his time to designing this book 'to help the cause of animal welfare'.

Thanks to my husband, Martin Humphery, not only for supporting me in my animal welfare work all these years but for joining me, now running an animal charity himself.

And thanks to all my friends who have supported our fundraising events, donating not only cash but cakes, too.

A proportion of the money raised from the sales of this book will go to my animal charities.

IT WASN'T CURIOSITY THAT KILLED THE CAT – IT WAS APATHY!